Democratic Accommodations

Democratic Accommodations: Minorities in Contemporary India

Peter Ronald deSouza

Hilal Ahmed

Mohd. Sanjeer Alam

B L O O M S B U R Y

NEW DELHI • LONDON • OXFORD • NEW YORK • SYDNEY

BLOOMSBURY INDIA
Bloomsbury Publishing India Pvt. Ltd
Second Floor, LSC Building No. 4, DDA Complex, Pocket C – 6 & 7,
Vasant Kunj New Delhi 110070

First published in India 2019
This paperback edition published 2025

Bloomsbury Academic
An imprint of Bloomsbury Publishing Plc

ISBN: PB: 978-93-69528-585-; eBook: 978-9-3884-1456-2

2 4 6 8 10 9 7 5 3 1

Typeset in Minion Pro by Manipal Digital Systems
Printed and bound in India by Manipal Technologies Limited, Manipal

To

Jawaharlal Nehru, who established the architecture
for a plural and inclusive India

To

Jawaharlal Nehru, who established the architecture
for a plural and inclusive India

Contents

List of Tables

List of Boxes

List of Abbreviations

AIMMM	All India Muslim Majlis-e-Mushawarat
AIMPLB	All India Muslim Personal Law Board
BJP	Bharatiya Janata Party
BMMA	Bharatiya Muslim Mahila Andolan
CA	Constituent Assembly
CABE	Central Advisory Board of Education
CAD	Constituent Assembly Debate
CBCI	Catholic Bishops' Conference of India
CMP	Common Minimum Programme
CP	Central Provinces
CPI	Communist Party of India
FGM	female genital mutilation
JUH	Jamiat Ulema-e-Hind
MCD	Minority Concentrated District
MHRD	Ministry of Human Resource Development
MoMA	Ministry of Minority Affairs
MsDP	Multi-sectoral Development Programme
NCF	National Curriculum Framework
NCM	National Commission for Minorities
NCMEI	National Commission for Minority Educational Institutions
NCRLM	National Commission for Religious and Linguistic Minorities
NIC	National Integration Council
NMDFC	National Minorities Development and Finance Corporation
NPE	National Policy on Education
NRC	National Register of Citizens
NSSO	National Sample Survey Organization

OBC	Other Backward Classes
RSS	Rashtriya Swayamsewak Sangh
SC	Scheduled Castes
SCR	Sachar Committee Report
SRC	States Reorganization Commission
ST	Scheduled Tribes
TG	transgender
UCC	Uniform Civil Code
UPA	United Progressive Alliance

Foreword

India's attitude to and treatment of its minorities has several unusual features that distinguish it from other plural democracies. It recognises many languages. There are national holidays for different religions, a relatively rare event in other societies. Dress, food and other such markers of cultural identity provoke no controversy. Minorities are constitutionally recognised and given clearly defined rights and liberties that are in some cases greater than those of the majority. Indeed, while they are a constitutional presence, the majority is hardly mentioned in the Constitution and hovers over it as a kind of pervasive but vague presence. All this needs to be explained. I suggest that the explanation is to be found in the formation of the Indian state, its non-ideological character and its hospitality to diversity.

In Europe, the birth of the state was a pretty violent affair involving the dismantling of the existing communities, expelling aliens, suppressing dissidents and creating a homogeneous space for the newly emergent state based on the supremacy of the dominant ethnos. The latter defined the identity of the state, saw itself as its historical bearer and set the norms to decide what was to be tolerated in the practices of its citizens. India followed a different path. The colonial rule which consolidated and designed the shape of the new state after much violence by and large made its peace with the existing ethnic, religious and other communities and made them its partners. The state made its own laws but also recognised those obtaining in the various communities. At Independence India had little choice but to continue with the prevailing arrangements. It had to reassure its minorities that they would continue to enjoy broadly the same degree of freedom and autonomy after independence as before. Had it not done so it would have created an even greater chaos than that surrounded its violent birth.

There was also another dimension to the state formation in India. Unlike Europe where the state established its own independent identity and enjoyed unchallenged supremacy over other bodies, especially the religious and the ethnic, the Indian state shared its sovereignty with them. The state was superior to them all but not supreme or sovereign in the European sense. In certain clearly designated areas its authority was subject to their approval and could only be exercised in cooperation with them. The minorities were constitutional partners of the state, sharing its sovereignty and enjoying broadly the same foundational status.

Another factor also played an important part in giving the minorities dignity and status. From the nineteenth century onwards liberalism and democracy were the widely available bodies of thought in Europe. They had different origins and historical trajectories but they dealt with complementary areas of social and political life. They needed to be combined and that could be done in three ways, giving rise to three different kinds of political system. One might privilege liberalism, define democracy within its limits and establish a liberal or liberalised democracy as Hobbes, Locke, Kant and others did. Or one could do the opposite, allow democracy to set the limits of liberalism and arrive at democratic liberalism as Rousseau, de Tocqueville and other did. Or finally one could give them more or less equal importance, suitably reinterpret them and bring them into harmony as T.H. Green and other British idealists did.

Of the three, liberal democracy has been the most widely adopted system in Europe. Although, it takes different forms in different countries depending on their history, traditions and social structure, certain basic features are common to them all. European liberal democracy is individualist in its orientation, taking the individual as the ultimate and irreducible moral unit of society. Individuals are deemed to be rational beings, basically equal, sharing a common human nature and seeking to lead free and self-chosen lives. They conduct their common affairs by debate, discussion and public reason, thereby allegedly making liberal democracy the most reflective and the highest level of collective existence. Citizens might belong to different religious, ethnic, linguistic and other communities but they are expected to transcend them when deliberating as citizens. Their primary identity is political, that of the citizen, and it trumps all others.

Every European state feels committed to this self-understanding and defines its identity in terms of it. It places great importance on such liberal values as critical rationality, equality, freedom, choice and personal autonomy and uses its interpretations of these values to approve or disapprove of minority practices. Some examples will clarify the point. A liberal democracy, we are told, not only should not but as a matter of principle 'cannot' allow gender inequality. This obviously would seem to mean women enjoying equality of rights with men. Does it also involve their feeling fully at ease with men? Rather strangely, it does in many European states. In Switzerland, a man refusing to shake hands with a female member of the interview board was denied citizenship. Something similar has happened in Sweden, and is being canvassed in Denmark. Again, can the 'hijab' be worn in public places? No, because it implies female subordination and refusal to integrate. Is this correct? Is it based on any survey? Could wearing the hijab not be a free choice of the women involved? No. Why? Because no European woman would want to restrict her freedom in this way. Could a muezzin use a loudspeaker to call the faithful to prayer? No, because it is a public nuisance and not a universal religious requirement. For whom is it a public nuisance? Not for the faithful surely. In all these and other cases the European woman, the contemporary European man and Christianity are uncritically turned into general public norms to which minorities are expected to conform. Since these are all controversial constructs based largely on local prejudices and none is truly universal, the resulting judgements have a parochial air. In European societies there is a systematic bias in favour of what is chosen, what is 'rational', and so on. This generates a persistent pressure towards uniformity and minority assimilation into the dominant structure of society. Liberalism is used as an ideological template, a kind of first premise from which appropriate policies and judgement emerge.

In India too both liberalism and democracy were widely available bodies of thought from the nineteenth century onwards introduced by the colonial rulers. They brought liberal ideas with them and introduced democracy incrementally in response to public demand or political exigencies. Given the nature of the colonial rule, the country opted for both and did not subordinate either to the other. Liberalism was important for its identity, but it was regulated and limited by democracy. Equally democracy was an important component of the political system but was subject to liberal limits. Democracy referred to 'the people' who, however, remained a complex and elusive entity. In India it included the religious, ethnic and other communities in which 'the people' were articulated. The people also included sub-communities or castes that were to be found in all communities, especially the Hindu majority. The term 'the people', thus, came to signify the totality of these communities and had a multi-communal character. The religious and ethnic minorities wanted the freedom to lead their customary ways of life. As for the castes, they demanded remedial and compensatory measures to overcome the handicap of centuries and improve their prospects. Liberty and justice were two of the central values towards which the Indian democracy was constitutionally committed.

India then, is not a liberal democracy sans phrase rather it is a liberally oriented multi-communal democracy. Both individuals and ethnic and religious communities lie at its basis, making it both an association of individuals and a community of communities. Since it sees itself as at least partly constituted in terms of communities, it has no difficulty respecting the customs and practices of its minorities so long as they are not patently unacceptable. Used to seeing differences as an integral part of life, those of dress, diet, ways of life and other markers of cultural and religious identity do not arrest Indian attention, let alone become spaces of confrontation. By making the minorities an explicit and valued constitutional presence, India has even given a new meaning to the term minority. The term does not refer to a small group living in the shadow of the majority, assigned an inferior status and expected over time to merge into the wider society, but rather to a historic group enjoying equality of status with the rest and enough power to prevent the majority from claiming to be the exclusive owner of the state. The various chapters in this book bring out this aspect very well, including the role of the courts in asserting the liberties and powers of the minority.

While the Indian state is respectful of minority practices, it is not so respectful of liberal values such as personal autonomy and freedom of speech that are often under threat from the collectivist pressures of democratic politics. One may not say anything likely to offend another's religious sensibility or critical of a past leader or someone's hero or cherished beliefs without incurring the wrath of the state or of the influential sections of public opinion. Again, the Indian state is inadequately sensitive to the internal oppressions within the minority communities. Sometimes it is simply not aware of them, more often it turns a blind eye to them or even positively endorses them. Such an attitude would be generally unacceptable in a European liberal democracy. While India has important lessons for Europe on the question of treating its minorities with respect, it also has much to learn from it in safeguarding and promoting important liberal values. A self-critical and open-minded dialogue between the two should help both.

In discussing India's treatment of its minorities from which other societies can learn much, one of the most important things to bear in mind is the rich composite culture that it has created and which has helped build bonds of trust and goodwill between the various communities and provided a framework in which to enjoy their commonalities and delight in their differences. This composite culture, sometimes referred to as unity in diversity or synthetic culture, is daily nourished by the creative contributions of India's Hindu, Buddhist, Muslim, Christian, secular Western and other streams of thought. Being the work of many hands, it has happily no single owner and forms the common heritage of them all. An Indian can hardly speak for long without resorting to his local language, Urdu and bits of English. Not only is his language plural, his ways of thinking too switch from one idiom to another. He draws on the great Muslim heritage when he wants to express romantic love, his English or Western heritage when he talks about civil, economic and political matters and on his rich Hindu heritage when he expresses his deepest moral, social and religious emotions.

Like the Indian civilisation itself, the Indian identity too is plural, multi-stranded and cannot be unidimensionally reduced to one of its constituents. All Indians carry within them various bits of Hindu, Muslim and other identities. No one is just a Hindu, he is also the bearer of non-Hindu identities which enable him to empathise and share a common life with others outside his fold. To exclude any of these is to impoverish and de-Indianise him. India's minorities do not represent the 'other', rather they are at the very heart of the Indian identity.

It is sad that in recent years Indians are beginning to show signs of moving away from the composite culture, especially in relation to the Muslims. Much of the anti-Muslim sentiment arises from a false reading of Indian history and a dubious view of the country's Partition. India was not partitioned along religious lines as is commonly argued, because that would have made it little more than a Hindu homeland. Rather, Pakistan was sliced off along religious lines, leaving India the multi-religious and multi-ethnic country that it has always been. This is one of the important messages of this fascinating book. With considerable skill, it analyses the ways in which successive Indian governments have developed various institutions and policies for accommodating its minorities within a democratic framework and facilitated their integration. Although, we need not worry about the rest of the world remaining indifferent to India's great experiment, we are right to feel that it would benefit greatly if it took greater interest. An outsider could not do better than start with this excellent book.

Bhikhu Parekh, FBA
House of Lords

Preface

Dealing with religious, cultural and other forms of diversity is an issue of vital concern for pluralistic democracies worldwide. Almost all societies in the contemporary world are becoming increasingly diverse in terms of the cultural and ethnic composition of their populations. As a result, governments are confronted with the challenge of shaping the way in which their societies deal with diversity. The interaction of different cultures and lifestyles often holds considerable potential for conflict that must be kept in check by rules ensuring peaceful coexistence.

In view of this cultural pluralisation, liberal democracies also face the challenge of ensuring equality and recognising the claims made by its minorities. These claims can include demands for special treatment of the marginalised groups or calls to fight discrimination and assuage insecurity, protect human rights and improve political participation and representation. All these claims require policy responses which recognise their legitimacy and acknowledge the value of diversity, but which also aim to integrate these different groups into the larger political community. Pluralistic democracies, in other words, must search for ways to establish and expand the common ground on which their diverse populations can live peacefully together.

Much of the debate on diversity so far has been focussing on the experience in North America and Europe. This means that the rich experience of societies in other regions of the world in dealing with religious, cultural and other minorities has been ignored or at least not given the attention it deserves. This also holds true for India, despite its abundant and instructive experience responding to claims from its various minority groups. The objective of this book is to change this situation and enhance the discourse on diversity by adding India's hitherto neglected perspective.

India is one of the most culturally and socially diverse countries in the world. It has a billion plus population, who belong to different languages, religions, castes, ethnicities and educational and socioeconomic backgrounds. The Constitution names 22 officially recognised languages many of which have their own script. The country is home to six main religions and innumerable smaller ones. A large majority of the over one billion Indians are Hindus. However, India also has the second largest population of Muslims in the world (only Indonesia has more). In addition, there are substantial communities of Sikhs, Christians, Buddhists and Jains. Adding even more complexity to the picture is caste or *jati* that is a principal identity for many people in India, defining whom they are expected to marry, associate with, vote for and fight against. These divisions of caste identities intersect with other cleavages based on language and religion as well as with the huge disparities in the distribution of wealth, income, education and class in the broader sense.

Given this unique cultural diversity and the associated social disparities, the renowned historian Ramachandra Guha has described India as an 'unnatural nation and unlikely democracy'. The forces that threatened India's unity were, and are, so manifold that he even raised the question, 'Why is there an India at all?' As the authors of this book point out, part of the answer lies in what they call the 'Indian model' of accommodating minorities. They show that since independence the dominant response of the Indian state when engaging with minority claims, has been a policy of accommodation, although this response has oscillated between a strong and active commitment to accommodation and a weak and more passive one. Moreover, they argue that this policy response has helped significantly in holding a huge and incredibly diverse country together.

This Indian experience of dealing with different minorities is important not only for India, but also for other countries as well. The Bertelsmann Stiftung has commissioned the research for this book in order to identify key issues that emerge from the Indian experience and to connect them to the larger global debate on diversity and minority claims in a democracy, especially those of religious and cultural minorities. The book is a follow-up project to the foundation's 2018 Reinhard Mohn Prize (RMP) that addressed this task under the title 'Living Diversity—Shaping Society', searching for impulses on how modern societies can live in peace and freedom under conditions of increasing diversity.

One of the key findings of the discussions at the RMP was that the preconditions for a functioning diversity could be divided into four dimensions: social inclusion, political participation, sense of belonging and interaction. Each of these dimensions underpins the normative concept of a pluralistic society in which all citizens exercise equal rights and freedoms in determining the body politic. The promise of a liberal democracy can only be fulfilled when everyone—regardless of their cultural identity—has equal access to opportunity (social inclusion), finds their interests represented in politics (political participation), feels connected to the social and cultural environment as a stakeholder (sense of belonging) and engages with others in the society on a regular basis (interaction).

While the authors of this book endorse the argument that all pluralistic democracies must work out strategies of accommodating minorities that are suited to the dynamics of their respective societies, they also present key learnings from the Indian experience that could be useful in this process. These learnings include the need to acknowledge diversity as a social and political reality and to establish specific institutions that respond to minority claims, the crucial role of the judiciary as the institution of last resort for resolving disputes, as well as the importance of encouraging the presence of minorities in the public sphere. We, therefore, hope that the rich and nuanced exploration of the Indian approach to the minority question presented in this book will, along with the book's conclusions, advance the international debate on diversity and multiculturalism and help policymakers in pluralistic democracies to develop their own particular strategies to deal with minority claims.

We wish to express our gratitude, first and foremost, to Peter Ronald DeSouza, Hilal Ahmed and Mohd. Sanjeer Alam for conducting the research and writing this book. We were fortunate enough to attract their unique expertise to this project, including their insights into the issues pertaining to minorities in India. Our special thanks also go to the Centre for the Study of Developing Societies (CSDS) and its director Sanjay Kumar for hosting a workshop on 23 October 2017 at its premises in New Delhi, that allowed for a discussion of an early draft of this publication. We also wish to thank all participants of this workshop for their comments and insights. Last but not the least, we are indebted to R. Chandra Sekhar for publishing this book at Bloomsbury.

This book will have met its purpose to the extent to which it contributes to a cross-cultural debate on diversity and minority claims. Given the various cultural conflicts and the ongoing political and societal polarisation across the world, such a debate is more important now than ever.

Stephan Vopel	**Peter Walkenhorst**
Director	Senior Project Manager
Program Germany and Asia	Program Germany and Asia
Bertelsmann Stiftung	Bertelsmann Stiftung

Acknowledgements

There are many individuals who have over the years contributed to our thinking about the place of minorities in Indian democracy. Not all of them are friends or colleagues or even contemporaries. Not all of them are alive or even aware of their contribution. Yet, we feel obligatory to begin our book with a tribute to them. The list begins with the famous, and not so famous, individuals of our freedom struggle. They campaigned for the idea of a plural India of which we are a part and from which we have gained. Our tribute now shifts to the members of India's Constitutional Assembly who gave this idea, its architecture and its moral grounding. This is the frame on which our modern nation is today being built amidst contestations that are both friendly and hostile. We would also like to acknowledge the many persons who, in Independent India, stood up for this diversity even at the cost of their lives. They gave birth to this project. Their arguments helped us frame the question of democratic accommodations that this book has sought to deliberate upon. In the first instance, therefore, we would like to thank all of them for giving this question a life. They are the giants upon whose shoulders we stand.

We must now move to the pleasant task of naming a few individuals and organisations who have endorsed this work.

We are grateful to Professor (Lord) Bhikhu Parekh for writing the 'Foreword'. By doing so, he has added his considerable thinking and arguments to our limited endeavour. He was very kind in accepting our request and did so without any hesitation.

We are also extremely grateful to the Bertelsmann Stiftung for financially supporting this project as a basis for a conversation between India and Europe. At different stages of the project, Peter Walkenhorst and Murali Nair helped in sharpening the arguments and making it aware of the different audiences that it could, and need to, think about and speak to.

We presented our initial findings, and tentative arguments, at a day-long workshop titled *The Minority Question in India* that was organised on 23 October 2017 at the Centre for the Study of Developing Societies (CSDS), New Delhi. This discussion helped us revisit our questions, sharpen our ideas, and present them in fuller form in this manuscript. We are grateful to all the participants, especially Zoya Hasan, Harsh Sethi, Irfanullah Khan, Surinder S. Jodhka, Rowena Robinson, Masooma Ranalvi, Maja Daruwala and Hemchandran Karah. We alone, however, bear responsibility for the arguments here.

This collaborative endeavour would not have been possible without the institutional support provided by CSDS—popularly known as the 'Centre' in the world of Indian social sciences. The work benefitted immensely from formal and casual conversations with our colleagues at the Centre. We express our deep gratitude to Ashis Nandy, D.L. Sheth, Shail Mayaram, Rajeev Bhargava, Sanjay Kumar, Aditya Nigam, Abhay Kumar Dubey, Awadhendra Sharan, Prathama Banerjee, Priyadarshini Vijaisri, Rakesh Pandey, Ravi Sundaram, Ravi Vasudevan, Ravi Kant and Ananya Vajpeyi for helping us position ourselves against their ideas often without their knowledge or consent. This is the spirit of the Centre.

We are also grateful to CSDS library and staff, Avinash Jha, Praveen Rai, Jaysree Jayanathan, K.A.Q.A. Hilal, Himanshu, Ghanshyam, Harsh, R. Natrajan, Jagdish, Ranjeet Negi, Manoj, Ayodhya Verma and others for their support.

Abhinav Srivastava and Syed Shahid contributed to this study by extending much-needed assistance for various aspects of the manuscript. We are thankful to them for their contribution.

We are glad to acknowledge the support that we received from our family members. Peter Ronald deSouza would like to thank his wife Ligia Noronha for the life of the mind she shared with him and for regularly, over several cups of evening tea, debating these ideas with him, and to his children Siddharth, Gayatri and Roshni for making him realise the value of the troublesome minority, a position he was often forced to occupy within the family. He is also grateful to Ralph Weber, from the University of Basel, for jointly examining with him the question of democracy's conundrums and for exploring the possibility of developing a 'political theory that matters'.

Hilal Ahmed would like to thank his wife Nazima Parveen for her intellectual role as a friend and partner, and his children—Sarmad, Maaz and Raheel for being supportive. A big thanks to Ayesha Pattnaik, Vishesh Guru, Mahima Sabherwal, Meher Sachdeva, Kairvy Grewal, Anirudh Rao—all from Ashoka University—for their comments and criticisms.

Mohd. Sanjeer Alam would like to thank his wife Hazra Sabeha for her love and support, especially in the moments when the chips are down; and his kids Shadab Ahmad and Shadma Sabeha who have just begun to encounter the term 'minority' in their school textbooks and classrooms which, in turn, has led them to ask difficult questions and to have a stimulating conversation on the same at home.

And finally, our sincere thanks to R. Chandra Sekhar, Publisher, Bloomsbury, New Delhi, for publishing this volume, and to the entire team at Bloomsbury for bringing it out without inordinate delay.

Peter Ronald deSouza
Hilal Ahmad
Mohd. Sanjeer Alam

Chapter 1

Introduction: Pluralism and Democracy

Assertive Pluralism

Most nation-states in the contemporary world are characterised by multi-ethnic and multicultural populations. Even the so-called monocultural nations have now to accept the social fact that they are characterised by a multi-ethnic and multicultural present that produces social dynamics they cannot ignore. There are communities within them that have either disagreed with the majority culture and have hence seceded from it,[1] or find it at variance from the one with which they have grown up, and hence consider it as a culture to be resisted. This social and demographic plurality has evolved because of many factors—long histories of changing or shifting territorial boundaries, occupation by foreign powers, growing economies especially after the Second World War where immigration was encouraged to meet labour needs, violent conflicts across the world from which people have fled, and most significantly, the legacies of colonial and imperial pasts. This last factor has given the erstwhile colonised people 'some claims'[2] against their colonial masters. It is a

[1] The Amish people in the United States are one example of a population that has seceded from the mainstream culture.

[2] These 'some claims' have rarely been studied yet they must be placed on the discussion table since they constitute rights claims that people from other lands can make in their new countries of residence. From passports with limited rights given to erstwhile residents of the colonies (e.g., British colonies of East Africa) to the right of residence for people from overseas provinces (Portuguese colony of Goa) to the right of return (Israel), these rights give a certain section of people claims arising from contested histories.

history that has produced new facts on the ground that is often neither recognised nor accepted[3] by the erstwhile colonisers (Osborn, 2002). The emergence of national populations with varying ethnocultural characteristics has, as a result of these various historical processes, exposed today's nations to a variety of issues.[4]

As this plurality unfolds across the world we see ethnic and cultural conflicts emerging that are a consequence of the politics among different groups of 'imagining the nation' and of integrating minority groups within the wider society. This produces contests between individual and group rights. There are demands for recognition of these differences and for according group rights due to such differences. There is the acknowledgement that the growing inequality between majority and minority groups, over time, has a cumulative character.

Nations have responded to this growing plurality in a variety of ways. The popular models adopted are of 'assimilation', 'integration' and 'multiculturalism'. Each model, wherever applied, has been marked by little success particularly since the last 20 years during which the children of immigrants, the third generation, are now making claims on citizenship. In this context of demands to recognise the differences the Indian model of 'accommodation' assumes significance. This book is aimed at what India (being one

[3] The British government's attitude to the immigrants from the West Indies who were brought over to England on the boat 'the Empire Windrush' is an example of both its ethical disingenuity and its truculence (*The Guardian*, 2018).

[4] The 14 April 2018 issue of *The Economist* of London had, as its lead editorial, a discussion on the new Germany. The blurb, at the start of the article, reads, 'Germany is becoming more open and diverse. With the right leadership it could be a model for the West.' The terms 'right leadership' and 'model for' should be regarded as keywords that any discussion on Germany's choices, as it faces the future, would need to think about. 'Leadership' refers not just to persons but also to forward-looking ideas and 'model' refers to a configuration of laws, institutions, policies and practices that regulate social life. Viewed thus, the elements of change that the article discusses make eminent sense. It describes the changes taking place in Germany where increasingly nationality is being defined 'in civic rather than ethnic terms', where the erstwhile patriarchal culture is becoming more 'gender balanced', where a cultural divide is opening up 'between those who embrace the new Germany and those who hanker for the familiar' and where the 'flow of new comers can cushion the demographic crunch'. A society that 'had long prized stability', the article observes, is being 'shaken up'. Germany is grappling 'with the rise of a more plural society'.

of the most ethnically and culturally diverse nations of the world) can offer to those nations, particularly to the countries of Europe, that are confronted with ethno-cultural and ethno-religious assertion and whose sociopolitical order is built on the principle of equality of citizens rather on granting them group-specific rights to minorities and on formulating policies to enable them to access resources and opportunities that are available to the wider society. Europe's settled order, it appears, is coming unstuck.

This study shows how history, context, law and politics have produced a certain institutional and policy discourse on the question of minorities within Indian democracy. It shows how the dominant narrative, concerning the state's response to minorities, has, in contrast to the European experience, been a policy of 'accommodation'. This response has oscillated between a strong and active commitment to 'accommodation' and a weak and passive one. Here we have endorsed the argument that all plural democracies—and all democracies can only be plural in the present historical conjuncture despite the attempts by regimes to make them majoritarian—must work out their own strategies of accommodation by evolving a policy matrix that is suited to the dynamics of their own societies. We have organised our discussion along four rubrics to help us understand Indian democracy's distinct response to diversity. These concern laws, institutions, policies and political discourse.

Innocuous But Not So Innocuous

Our starting observation here is that all nations, however small—think Fiji, or Sri Lanka or Sweden[5]—have to respond to an assertive

[5] Fiji experienced military coups in 1987 to sideline the ethnic Indian population. Sri Lanka went through a long and tragic civil war when the majority Sinhalese feared the demands of the Tamils particularly in the area of Jaffna. Even in Sweden which has had a progressive social democratic politics for decades, the right-wing populist party, the Sweden Democrats, came second garnering a high percentage of votes in the 9 September 2018 elections. This shows that the fear of immigrants has taken root in the liberal Swedish countryside (Orange, 18 December 2018).

plurality. They have to acknowledge the claims coming from their different citizen groups (migrant as well as native citizens) and from other minorities, who wish to see themselves as equal citizens in the public life of their country. For this to happen, assuming it is not yet the case, it would require that these claims—cultural, ethical and political—be accommodated. These are not straightforward claims. They pose ethical and political challenges. They extend from demands for the group to be given special treatment, to protection of minority rights, to steps to assuage insecurity, to initiatives to improve minority participation in politics and finally to recognise diversity as a part of the natural political order.

Making all these accommodations requires policy responses that aim to both integrate the groups within the larger political community while also simultaneously accepting their special claims and distinct status.[6] Such accommodation should not be the result of enlightened benevolence but the result of a genuine acceptance of the validity—which has to be established politically, legally and normatively—of these minority claims. It would require reworking the political and cultural coordinates of the new polity. Even in settled times—which the present times are not—this is not an easy exercise especially in competitive democracies where the political calculus is to create stable constituencies of support for partisan ends and where, therefore, denigrating minorities is an easier option.

Today's Europe is at an interesting intellectual and historical conjuncture. It has a great deal of learning to undertake on what accommodations to make and why, on the social dynamics produced by these accommodations, and on the gains and costs that follow

---

[6] One of the dimensions of this task of building a plural democracy is the challenge of dealing with religious minorities who can, in Rawlsian terms, be considered as existentially inhabiting different 'comprehensive doctrines'. Habermas too, in his work on 'Religion in the Public Sphere', has drawn attention to the cognitive asymmetry between secular and religious claims (Habermas, 2006, pp. 1–25). The challenge facing a plural democracy is, therefore, to build and expand the 'overlapping consensus' (Rawls, 1987, pp. 1–26) between these different groups within which the polity can establish its norms of co-living.

from them. To make our case of this growing assertiveness of groups and of the responses to them, we shall briefly look at the cultural and political landscape of Europe. It shows many contestations currently underway which may appear innocuous but are not really so for beneath the surface lie world views and cosmologies that are contested and that do not align easily with each other. The innocuous is not so innocuous.

The declining of a handshake offered in a school in Switzerland, an unremarkable episode by most standards, surprisingly produced a national controversy (deSouza, 2016). The place of Zwarte Pieten (Black Pete), who accompanies Sinterklaas in the Dutch celebration of Christmas, has generated an intense debate in Holland (Pleasance, 2014). The question of what should be the permitted swimwear, if any, for women on a French beach has divided French public opinion. These disputes have produced a language of public discussion with terms such as 'our culture' versus 'their culture', 'progressive' versus 'regressive' and 'women's freedom' versus 'women's subjugation' being bandied about (Dearden, 2016). In the United States, a soul searching debate is underway on how to respond to its slave-owning past. From Confederate statues to be retained or pulled down as memorials, to flags to be kept or discarded, to college crests to be abandoned (Ryan, 2018), a demand has arisen to change those symbols that apparently celebrate slavery.[7] At Yale University students started a movement to change the name of Calhoun College on the grounds that Calhoun was a slave owner. The present, they held, requires the university to take a position vis-à-vis a dark and oppressive past especially since students from minority African-American or coloured backgrounds felt humiliated by the name (Schuessler, 2016). After initial resistance, the name was changed and a policy which sets out the procedures to be adopted when faced with similar demands in the future was adopted. In Iceland, on the practice of circumcision, a public debate has grown

[7] It is interesting to compare the response of the two educational institutions Yale University and Oriel College Oxford University to a similar demand.

on whether it should be seen purely from a health perspective, and therefore proscribed, or be regarded as a religious practice at the heart of a community's self-definition, and should therefore be permitted? The argument gets further complicated when seen in gender terms. Is it all right for men to be circumcised because of religious practice but not for women where it is seen as gender unjust (Sherwood, 2018). The debate on circumcision in Iceland finally resulted in a court verdict banning the practice which in turn produced a global controversy (Hofverberg, 2018). Minority assertiveness on issues that were not part of the mainstream political discourse, that were perhaps even lying dormant and regarded as insignificant, have now, as a result, entered the public sphere. Are these just expressions of cultural difference or of incommensurable comprehensive doctrines?

This brief survey shows that each issue has the potential to become a site for political struggle. Each requires that the ethical, political, religious and cultural aspects of the case be examined. It is clear from these contestations that what is at stake are citizen's rights in a democracy. To help us navigate this turbulence we feel it necessary to draw on the resources of political theory, where concepts such as 'overlapping consensus', 'comprehensive doctrines', 'public reason', 'minority rights', 'deliberative processes' and 'cultural pluralism' are offered (Fraser, 1990; Habermas, 2006; Kymlicka, 1992; Rawls, 1987; Zerilli, 2012). We have flagged these concepts here to gesture to a literature that must be examined as we try to craft rules for co-living in plural democracies. Parallel processes must take place simultaneously, arguments on what should be the normative principles for a plural society and the pragmatics of accommodation and coalition building.

We can also draw on the experience of countries outside Europe where innovative responses to the emerging and assertive plurality are tried. South Africa, for example, pioneered the institution of the Truth and Reconciliation Commission as it sought to rebuild its rainbow nation from the trauma of apartheid.[8] This had implications for the

[8] http://www.justice.gov.sa/trc/report/index.htm (accessed 12 July 2018).

judicial system and for the social process of attending to the pain of the victims in post-conflict contexts. Kenya, in 2017, gave tribal status to Asians, as the 44th tribe of the country to deepen their sense of belonging as equal citizens (Mwere, 2017). Giving Asian Kenyans a tribal status is an interesting innovation of acknowledging diversity and granting citizenship rights in plural societies. Canada continues to struggle with what seems to be a simple issue, the question of giving an official name to a group, which it appears is not so simple as it shifts from calling its indigenous people 'Indians', as it did earlier but the term today is considered offensive. Now it refers to them as the peoples of the First Nations (Parrott, 2007). This can be seen as a change of name which is reflective of a changed public discourse that is more accommodative of the demands of these minority groups demanding greater dignity and equality of rights. These national gestures can all be seen as moving plural societies in the direction of a decent society.[9]

Fortunately, for this study, India is available as a valuable case for deeper study. It has responded to its own assertive plurality by enacting laws, creating institutions, formulating policies and nurturing a political discourse that constitutes a rich archival lode of material for examination. In the discussion that follows we shall look at the efforts of the postcolonial democratic state in India as it negotiates this plurality. Our focus will be primarily on language and religion. The building of a modern Indian state required inspired leadership and inspired thinking. In the early years, India had both in abundance which was deployed with considerable creative energy. What follows is a record of this effort.

This study is organised into five chapters. The first and introductory chapter looks through a political theory lens at some contestations in both India and Europe. We expect to flag issues that must be considered by policy communities across democracies and, by doing

---

[9] The concept of a 'decent' society has considerable purchase and requires more attention at the high table of political philosophy (Margalit, 1996).

so, alert them to the many layers from the ethical to the political that are involved in the dispute. The second and third chapters take us on a detailed journey through the politics of independent India as it sets up the architecture of the modern state and as it negotiates its way through laws, institutions, policies and discourses. The fourth focuses specifically on the policy responses—cultural, educational, social justice and affirmative—that the Indian state adopts to meet the aspiration for equal citizenship among its minorities. The fifth and final chapter draws together all the issues that have been signposted to offer some suggestions for more detailed discussion. It also briefly looks at the recent accommodations that have been made towards sexual minorities.

Some Conceptual Issues

We would like to begin this discussion by referring to the reflections on the minority question by the first Prime Minister of independent India, Jawaharlal Nehru. His is a legacy that, unfortunately, is being undermined by the regime that has been in power in the latter part of the second decade of the twenty-first century. Nehru saw the task of building the architecture of a modern state as one of the main tasks of his premiership. He was obsessed with the protection and enabling features that had to be established to give a reality to the Fundamental Rights and Directive Principles spelt out in the Constitution. One can discern this obsession in his fortnightly letters to the Chief Ministers (deSouza, 2015). Here, he expressed himself on the different issues confronting the new India. They could be of a minor nature, such as the question of posting a married couple in the foreign services to the same location, or a more philosophical question on the need to develop a scientific temper in India to address the problem of poverty, ignorance and superstition. As a child of the enlightenment, he invested in the liberal promise of equal rights for all citizens. He believed that societal progress would take place through science and technology and through the commitment to reason.

On the issue of minorities he wrote in a letter on 16 January 1956, less than six years after India became a Republic:

> Minorities may be, and sometimes have been, troublesome and have made exaggerated claims. In a democracy, however, it is the will of the majority that ultimately prevails. The responsibility, therefore, rests on the majority to not just do justice to the minority but, what is more important, to win over the goodwill and confidence of the minority group, whether it is linguistic, religious or other. (Nehru, 1992, p. 336)

Reading this passage 63 plus years after it was written and at a time in global politics when the minority is indeed under stress, we find several issues that are of concern to us and that, irrespective of whether Nehru intended the meanings that we wish to draw from them or not, speak to our contemporary concerns. Let us, therefore, try and examine them through a political theory lens so that we can flag some themes for the subsequent elaboration of India's story of accommodation.

The first is the idea of a 'troublesome' group that makes 'exaggerated claims'. 'Troublesome' here could refer to the unsettling nature of the claim made by the minority. This is a claim that needs to be addressed by the democratic state both on pragmatic grounds because it shares a common political space with the majority, a space which must be kept peaceful, and on ethical grounds because of the common obligation to nurture and sustain a constitutional morality. It is troublesome because accommodating the claim would require engaging with its ethical premises and in doing so working towards a decision on whether to accept or reject, wholly or partially, the claim being made. Reasons for the decision would have to be given. This is ordinarily a cumbersome process.[10]

[10] The BBC programme 'Crossing Divides' (2018) shows the challenges of such a conversation.

'Troublesome' could also refer to the fact that accommodation would mean changing the normative and political coordinates of the polity which serve as beacons to guide the polity. These have been achieved through long historical struggles by groups within the polity. There is, therefore, resistance to change. For example, a call has to be taken on whether accommodating the new minority claim diminishes the gains of the earlier historical struggle—such as, the Hijab and women's dress—or in fact strengthens them. While the observation of 'exaggerated claims' can be read as being a statement of fact it also refers to epistemic differences between the majority and the minority. From the viewpoint of the majority the minority claim is exaggerated for example, carrying a *kirpan* (a small knife with a cover which Sikhs are required to carry as a symbol of their faith) on a flight, whereas from the perspective of the minority it is perfectly reasonable (BBC, 2017). The two groups see the world differently and, therefore, reconciling their core concerns is not easy.[11]

The feeling that the minority makes exaggerated claims is growing in both Europe and India as minorities make their demands for recognition not just of their claims (which are often in the nature of religious or cultural claims) but also for the acceptance of these claims. These may be at variance with majority practices or may be offensive to them or even worse they might be in opposition to them. The minority uses the liberal promise of protection of rights (both

---

[11] Bhikhu Parekh, in 'Minority Practices and Principles of Toleration', argues that

> if the impasse persists the values of the wider society should prevail for at least three reasons: (i) they are woven into its institutions and practices, form part of the lived social reality, and cannot be changed without causing considerable moral and social disorientation; (ii) while a society has an obligation to accommodate an immigrant's way of life, it has no obligation to do so at the cost of its own especially when it is both able to make out a reasonably good case for its values and remains genuinely unconvinced by the minority's defence of the disputed practice; and (iii) since immigrants are new to the wider society's way of life they need to appreciate that its nature and inner workings are likely to elude them and that they should defer to its judgment on doubtful matters. (Parekh, 1996, pp. 251–284)

individual and group) and on the defence of a plural democracy.[12] These claims, they argue, are not just in the interests of the minority but are also in the interests of the majority since they concern the constitutional promise of equal citizenship.[13]

The second idea that can be extracted from Nehru's statement is that 'in a democracy the will of the majority shall ultimately prevail', and that this *will* carries a 'responsibility' not to impose its own perspective, or to neglect the standpoint of the minority but to act in such a manner that it does 'justice' to minority concerns (Walzer, 1990). What is entailed by such 'justice'? Is there some universal position from which justice is defined or is justice always seen only from a particular location: of the majority, of the minority, of the established, of the new? This is a vexed question and has been at the centre of political theory debates on whether ethical relativism is what we have to accept or whether we can, in practice, settle disputes by relying on a strategy of what Dworkin (1997) calls 'justificatory ascent'?[14] Does it require wholesale acceptance, minor adjustment,

[12] John Rawls in his classic work *Political Liberalism* (1993) in the chapter on 'The Idea of an Overlapping Consensus' states seven facts of modern democracies: (i) the fact of pluralism; (ii) the fact of permanence of pluralism given the democratic institutions; (iii) the fact that agreement on a single comprehensive doctrine presupposes the oppressive use of state power; (iv) the fact that an enduring and stable democratic regime, one not divided into contending factors and hostile classes, must be willing and freely supported by a substantial majority by, at least, its politically active citizens; (v) the fact that a comprehensive doctrine whenever widely, if not universally, is shared in society, tends to become oppressive and stifling; (vi) the fact that reasonably favourable conditions (administrative, economic, technological and the like) which make democracy possible exist and finally (vii) the fact that the political culture of a society with a democratic tradition implicitly contains certain fundamental intuitive ideas from which it is possible to work up a political conception of justice for a constitutional regime.

[13] 'The political and theoretical problem this social and cultural pluralism produces is how to set fair terms of social cooperation among groups who diverge in their conception of the good, in such a way that no reasonable conception of the good is oppressed or restricted' (Young, 1995, p. 186).

[14] 'But justificatory ascent is always, as it were, on the cards: we cannot rule it out a priori because we never know when a legal claim that suddenly seemed pedestrian and even indisputable may suddenly be challenged by a new and potentially revolutionary attach from a higher level' (Dworkin, 1997, p. 357).

considerable accommodation or, in the last instance, a demand to assimilate and integrate?[15]

The challenge plural democracies face is, therefore, to develop a 'public will' through a deliberative process which, when it prevails, is accommodative of the reasonableness of minority claims.[16] The challenge is to move the public mind from a disposition that seeks to impose to one that accepts, defends and normalises the pluralistic character of society. Public education in schools and discussions in public fora are needed to be able to successfully effect that change in the public mind.[17] There will be resistance here since norms of co-living that have been taken for granted, accepted as valuable and settled, will now have to be revisited. What had become routinised will now demand cognitive attention on grounds of fairness. It will require ethical repositioning of the polity. This is not a political path that can be avoided. Plural societies periodically require such re-calibration.

The third idea from Nehru's statement that is worth considering is the injunction to 'win over the goodwill of the minority group'. The suggestion here is that the minority group even if it is composed of recent migrants from alien cultures or represents hitherto suppressed

---

[15] In history majorities have responded to minorities by either acts of genocide and ethnic cleansing (as took place against the Jews in Nazi Germany) or expulsion (Pandits in Kashmir or Christians in Iraq by ISIS) or suppression (Kurds in Turkey) or intimidation (Hindus in Pakistan and Bangladesh or Copts in Egypt) or exclusion (Roma people in Europe and Tamil People in Sri Lanka) or by demanding integration and assimilation as is happening in France with respect to its Maghrebian communities.

[16] Every contemporary democracy is a divided nation.... We are divided culturally, ethnically, politically and morally. We nevertheless aspire to live together as equals, and it seems absolutely crucial to that ambition that we aspire that the principles under which we are governed treat us as equals.... We cannot pursue that indispensable ambition unless we undertake, where necessary, to ascend enough in our collective deliberations, including our adjudicative deliberations, to test our progress in that direction. We must undertake that sovereign duty if we claim a rule of law that is not just an instrument for economic achievement and social peace, but an emblem and mirror of the equal public regard that entitles us to claim community. (Dworkin, 1997, p. 376)

[17] The case of the Italian Mayor in Riace who welcomed immigrants and thereby stemmed depopulation in the town and revived it but is now facing prosecution for his actions is an instructive case of conflict between the two perspectives (Momigliano 2018).

groups or stands for groups that challenge settled rules of co-living needs to be given access to political spaces within institutions and within the public sphere that would allow it to articulate its views and to feel that its viewpoint has been given serious consideration by the majority before a public decision that is binding on all is taken.[18] This is not to suggest that winning over is easy especially in a competitive democracy where 'majority making' is the primary goal of political parties and where troublesome minorities led by social elites from within the community, or by religious leaders who want to preserve orthodoxy in the face of modernity, refuse to be won over (Sheth, 2009). There is little desire to develop and expand an 'overlapping consensus' (Rawls, 1987). If neglecting the minority or being hostile to them can give electoral dividends as has been the case in India since 2014, and in much of Europe today, then political parties will ignore minority demands. Nehru's call for winning over is not based on strategic thinking, which comes from an electoral calculus, but is instead rooted in the ethical idea of a Republic that is strong only in its nurtured plurality. In such a context winning over the goodwill of the minority requires patience, imagination and political statesmanship. These are in short supply in India today where 'majority making', especially a muscular majority, is the driver of politics. They were, however, available in abundance in the Nehruvian period of the 1950s and 1960s.

These three issues of 'troublesome minority', 'responsibility of the majority' and 'winning over the goodwill of the minority' are issues that are alive in the plural societies of Europe and India. Conflict

---

[18] Here, Nancy Fraser in her work 'Rethinking the public sphere' sets out four aspects of pushing forward this project of accommodation: (i) Open access, participation parity and social equality; (ii) equality, diversity and multiple public; (iii) public spheres, common concerns and private interests and (iv) strong and weak public. Fraser argues in response to the difficulty of intercultural communication that 'communication across of lines of difference is not in principle impossible … granted such communication requires multi-cultural literacy, but that can be acquired through practice. In fact, the possibilities expand once we acknowledge the complexity of cultural differences' (Fraser, 1990, p. 69).

situations emerge at unexpected places. They range from the trivial to the more enmeshed aspects of group life, to the core aspects of community identity. By looking at cases from India and Europe let us now examine such contestations and the response to them.

Claims and Contestations

Let us begin with what appears to be a trivial example. In France, recently a dispute broke out over menus for school children and whether pork should be a part of such menus (Chrisafis, 2015). Children were earlier given a choice between a pork dish or a chicken/turkey dish but with the emergence of some mayors who have political leanings towards the right-wing National Front school meals have become the site for political battles in some local governments. By arguing for the uniformity of school meals these authorities want minorities to assimilate into the majority French culture. Eating pork, it is argued, is a core aspect of French culture. We have called this conflict trivial since the solution is easy and does not need to become a political dispute. The practice, before it became an issue, was to offer the children a choice of menus so that their religious preferences could be accommodated. This would give them both a sense of belonging to the large society and at the same time being a part of a different community within it. But majority assertion in some regions of France, according to *The Guardian* report, has exacerbated this conflict into a zero-sum game, where the majority gains and the minority loses. Eat pork on days when it is served or go hungry is the policy of those city governments controlled by the National Front. Mothers of minority children have reported being distressed at having to choose between their children remaining hungry because of taboo foods or eating and transgressing religious injunctions.

A second more enmeshed conflict is the statement by the Chief Inspector of Ofsted that, '…Under the pretext of religious belief, they (referring to minorities) use education institutions, legal and illegal, to narrow young people's horizons, to isolate and segregate, and in the worst cases to indoctrinate impressionable minds with extremist ideology' (Adams, 2018). The issue concerned a decision by the head of a school in the UK to prohibit children below the age of eight from wearing hijabs since it would amount to sexualising them before they had reached puberty. This, she believed, was unacceptable. The case only concerned girls below the age of eight. In response, the minority community protested the decision and campaigned against the head of the school who was accused of discrimination. In this case, there was little scope for 'winning over' the minority since they had in fact, escalated the conflict by asking for the head of the school to be dismissed. Here, we see minority intransigence where fixed interpretations of the practice are offered and negotiation is ruled out. In such contestations, sometimes, minority intransigence is an obstacle to working out the rules of co-living. Often in our eagerness to resist majority tyranny we do not equally criticise minority inflexibility and are, therefore, seen by the majority as being less than even-handed.[19] Minorities must be willing to revisit positions that they had considered inviolate if they wish to live as equal citizens in a plural society. Accommodation is a two-way street. In the extant case, the news reports illustrate the rigidity of minorities. One could perhaps interpret this rigidity as the strategy of minority elites to consolidate their hold over the community, to be considered as the legitimate voice of the community. This is often a conservative voice that is being resisted by minorities within minorities who have to often face the threat of social ostracism by the community or of being told not to break ranks (Kirmani, 2011).

The third class of conflicts is a straightforward clash of values. Here, there is little public uncertainty about which side to support and which to oppose. This clarity has come because of a shared consensus among groups, won over time and over many struggles, on the public value of 'gender equality'. The history of Modern India is replete with

---

[19] This perception of political correctness is producing a push back by the majority community.

such struggles from which the constitutional order has evolved. The case concerns the challenge by women's groups of the patriarchal rules debarring women from entering places of worship, such as at the Haji Ali Dargah in Mumbai or the Shani Shingnapur temple in Ahmednagar. The protesting group of women entered both the areas that were prohibited to women and worshipped there in the same manner as men were doing. There was resistance from a few men but such resistance enjoyed little public support and certainly not from the major political players who felt that it would cost them more in terms of women's votes to oppose the temple entry. Electoral democracy became the decider here. The deepening of gender rights and gender justice in India has been the result of such struggles by women's groups. The action undertaken by the women activists to enter prohibited areas was later endorsed by the courts. However, the October 2018 decision of the Supreme Court of India to allow women to worship in the Sabarimala temple, where women of menstruating age were hitherto prohibited, has divided society not on gender lines alone but also on the issue of legitimate/illegitimate interference with tradition. In fact, soon after the judgement the police had to escort women who tried to worship at the temple. Their attempts were unsuccessful and were met with fierce public opposition (Chatterjee, 2018; Raina, 2018).

The fourth set of cases is more complicated since they initially appear to be low profile, even innocuous, but soon acquire a certain voltage when one discovers that what is, in fact, taking place is a clash of fundamental values that are important to the two sides. Compromise and accommodation here become more difficult. The case in Germany on circumcision, for example, illustrates the point. When a Higher Regional Court in Cologne in 2012 decided that religious circumcision of boys constituted 'bodily harm' and ruled that a 'child's right to self-determination superseded his parent's right to freedom of religion' it caused not just a national uproar with Muslim and Jewish groups protesting interference by the state in religious matters, but a global controversy in which Turkey and Israel joined the issue (Wagner, 2011). This is similar to the public discussion in India where activists of the group *Speak Out on FGM* (female genital mutilation) have campaigned against female circumcision among Dawoodi Bohras (Ranalvi, 2017).

In this debate, in fact, there are so many levels. Is FGM religiously sanctioned? Is it an essential religious practice? Do the community authorities support it? Do opponents face social sanction? And even how to name the procedure, that is, should it be called Female Genital Mutilation or just Female Genital Cutting? This controversy on naming is because the use of the word 'mutilation', some argue, leaves the victim with a permanent sense of physical deficit (a double punishment, physical and psychological) which should be avoided. But then avoiding the word diminishes the extent of the trauma that is visited on minor girls thereby lessening its severity in the public discourse (WHO, 2016). This simple case shows that a small issue that belongs to the cultural and religious world of a minority community soon becomes a major issue of constitutional morality concerning, for example, the equal right to religious practice versus the equal right of protection from bodily harm, or the best interests of the child versus minority rights (Convention on the Rights of the Child, UNICEF, 2018). This debate of the fundamental values that should undergird a plural polity takes place within a progressive discourse on gender justice.

The fifth class, similar to the fourth, but less innocuous and more public, concerns core issues of minority identity and can be considered as belonging to those conflicts that can be described as a clash of comprehensive world-views. In this, we would include the debate on the different personal laws of minority communities in India. The 23 August 2017 judgement of the Supreme Court on the practice of Triple Talaq[20] by the minority Muslim community shows how even a five-member bench was split three ways on

[20] Triple Talaq is a practice among the minority Muslim community in which a man divorces his wife. It involves saying 'talaq' (I divorce you) three times in one go thereby ending the marriage. Although this practice is rarely resorted to, there have been cases in the recent past where men have used this option of the triple talaq to divorce their wives. The divorced women approached the courts, that is, the secular authority for relief and protection of their rights guaranteed by the constitution.

what it regarded as the fundamental grounds for either striking down or retaining the community practice of Triple Talaq (Bhatia, 2017; Vijayan, 2017). Questions such as the following can be seen as emerging from the judgement: (a) Should a secular institution be the final arbiter of religious practices and laws? (b) For a free society committed to religious freedom does the court's intervention constitute interference in the individual's inviolable area of religious freedom or is such intervention permitted, or even necessary, in rare cases? (c) Should reforms of personal laws be promoted only from within the community or can they also be imposed from outside by external authority, the constitutional democratic state, when required? These are not easy questions but they need to be asked if the polity is to be able to deal fairly with minority claims. The judgement of the Supreme Court was one response to the contested question and after it was given we had to decide whether to endorse only the procedure of adjudication followed or also the substance of the judgement itself. Plural democracies will have to deal as part of its normal life with such clashes of comprehensive world-views (Sandel, 1994).

These five classes of conflicts are a normal feature of plural democracies because the core promise of democracy is to give the group a voice to make claims and to articulate demands. There are many aspects of these cultural conflicts that need to be investigated such as: (a) the issue of 'minorities within minorities' whose claims are often ignored in the desire to accommodate the big minority's claim (Pfaff-Czarnecka, 2010); (b) or rights of migrant citizens contrasted with the rights of native citizens (Gole, 2015); (c) or the politics of recognition and politics of identity that has increasingly become a feature of democratic mobilisation (Tully, 2000); (d) or the issue of designing political systems where power can be shared between groups (Lijphart, 2004);[21] and finally (e) the key conceptual issue of

[21] 'Power sharing denotes the participation of representatives of all significant communal groups in political decision making especially at the executive level. Group autonomy means that these groups have autonomy to run their own affairs especially in the areas of education and culture' (Lijphart, 2004, p. 97).

the relation between individual rights and community rights and the determination of which gets precedence in a situation of a contest (Etzioni, 2014). It will not be possible for us to discuss these aspects in detail here since they cover a vast literature. We have flagged them here primarily to place them on the discussion agenda, to point to the various responses given to them when we are looking for arguments to deal with our own conundrums and to recognise their salience for plural democracies.

Who is a Minority?

At this stage, it is perhaps necessary for us to offer a working definition of what we mean by a minority. The first aspect is that the concept of minority is a relational concept. It refers to a group whose existence is defined by its relation with another group which is a majority. The second aspect refers to a group that is mostly in a non-dominant position with respect to its culture but that seeks to protect its cultural distinctiveness—which may be religious, linguistic, sexual or ethnic—by seeking acceptable terms of recognition for this distinctiveness from the larger society. What these terms are, or should be, is the basis for negotiation with other groups.

In world history, the relationship between the majority and the minority has been fraught and tendentious as the majority itself seeks to produce cultural and normative homogeneity within the emergent nation-state and hence the contrasting claims of the minority produce a discordance that is troublesome. Unable and unwilling to deal with minority claims the majority has historically relied on pogroms, genocide, suppression, and more recently, in many countries of Europe, demand for integration and assimilation into the majority culture, defined as that which the dominant group says it is.

In India, till recently, the response has been one of gradual accommodation of minority claims. While a discursive journey across the globe would certainly be instructive (Kymlicka, 2008a) this study looks only at India. In the South Asian context, India looks pretty in contrast to Afghanistan, Pakistan, Bangladesh, Sri Lanka, Nepal and even the Maldives (Khan and Rahman, 2009), as to how it has dealt with minority claims by relying on law, institutions, policies and politics (deSouza, 2018). In what follows we shall track this journey. It shows how a combination of visionary leadership, political sagacity and pragmatism produced a democratic politics of accommodation. It also shows how this journey has not been linear with moments of reversal, such as the present period, and then again followed by moments of advance. The following chapters will begin with the late pre-colonial period where the idea of a minority emerged in the Indian political discourse because of the instruments of governance deployed by the colonial state. It will then move to the postcolonial period as laws, institutions and non-party political formations representing minorities emerged as democracy expanded and demands were conceded on both prudential and ethical grounds. It will close by looking at the policy realm where the state attempted policy interventions in many areas from the cultural such as making religious holidays as giving scholarships to minority students from deprived and disadvantaged backgrounds. It is an interesting journey from which plural democracies across the globe can profitably draw valuable comparisons and useful lessons.

Chapter 2

Emerging Idea(s) of the Minority in Colonial India

From flagging the normative and political issues that emerge in plural societies when minorities make claims we shall now move to discussions of the place of minorities in modern Indian history. We shall trace the different official ways by which the expression 'minority' was conceived, articulated, defined and communicated. The purpose here is not to produce a political history of the 'minority/majority' relationship in modern India but instead to offer a context-specific analysis of the evolving architecture of the state in India both in the colonial period and, in a later chapter, in the postcolonial period. This chapter is written in the belief that normative discussions, outlined in the previous chapter, must be read alongside the historical details of state making to appreciate how decisions were made. This is especially important where such modern institutions have to be crafted and given legitimacy by various publics.

Colonial Knowledge and the Production of Minority/Majority Framework

The colonial regime—the East India Company as well as the British state of India —relied heavily on its 'knowledge producing techniques' such as the conduct of the census, the organisation of land records, the research on religion, culture and history of the native population, the codification of personal laws, etc. to administer the Empire. Although it would be a simplification to reduce this 'quest for knowledge' to the direct political interest of governing the colony, it is important to recognise the significant role of colonial knowledge in producing a new language of politics in India.[1] Hence expressions such as 'minority' and 'majority'—as legitimate official categories to describe, classify and interpret Indian social groups in clear numerical terms—can be seen to have their genesis in the logic of the colonial state.

The colonial knowledge apparatus, through the census, produced statistical data with regard to the socio-geographical landscape of Indian social groups. In this process, religious groups such as Hindus, Muslims, Christians, Sikhs and Parsis became distinct populations within India's social and political reality.[2] This scientific exercise of data collection had its own logic. At one level, the numerically larger population came to be known as the 'majority' while the numerically smaller population was referred to as a 'minority', that is, Hindus as a majority and non-Hindus (mainly Muslims and Sikhs) as minorities. The data set of Hindus as a majority, for instance, could only be understood in relation to the non-Hindu data set of Muslims as a minority.[3] The majority–minority idea was, therefore, essentially relational.

The Census Report of 1891 is a good example. It makes very crucial and powerful observations about Indian communities seeing Muslims as the adherents of a pan Islamic community and also as a numerically inferior group in India in contrast to the Hindus, who were described as the original inhabitants of the country and who were seen as a majority. Further, it defines Hinduism and Islam as two conflicting religious traditions noting:

> The … form of creed, under the title of Hinduism, is returned by more than 72 per cent, of the population of India …. Primarily and

[1] Arjun Appadurai makes this clarification. He argues that in colonial India *numbers* had two aspects—the justificatory and the disciplining (Appadurai, 1989; emphasis added).

[2] The point here is that the concepts not only mirror reality but also create it.

[3] This is an elaboration of the point made in the first chapter. See also Kaviraj (1997).

> historically, it is the antithesis of Islam, and thus includes all Indian forms of faith in which the uncompromising Unitarianism of the adherents of the Prophet detected signs of the worship of idols .... The next religion to come under review is that of Islam, which is taken here on account of its numerical importance. The Musalman population of the world has been roughly estimated at various amounts from 70 to 90 million, so that whatever the real figure may be between those limits, the Indian Empire contains a large majority of the followers of the Prophet. No Province or large State, and probably few districts or other subdivisions in the plain country west of Burma, is without a certain number of Musalman inhabitants. (Baines, 1893, pp. 158–174)

This straightforward classification of Indian religious groups as populations also functioned differently at another level of knowledge production. By the early nineteenth century, the colonial historical researchers produced an equally powerful discourse of 'authentic' India. The Hindus were seen as the old, natural and authentic habitants of this land as all their revered places of worship were situated in the geopolitical entity called the 'Indian subcontinent'. The Muslims, the numerically second most powerful group and who had also been the rulers of this land before the British were considered to be outsiders. The scope of this 'authentic India theory' was further expanded to answer difficult questions such as: Why did Hindus as a collectivity fail to protect their land despite being a majority in medieval India? Or, why were there no grand Hindu temples in the regions where Muslim rule flourished?

James Mill's famous book, *The History of British India* (1826) might be taken as a point of departure to understand the significance of these questions within the dominant colonial imagination of India. It is worth noting that Mill was the first official British historian who divided Indian history into three periods: the ancient as Hindu, the medieval as Muslim, and the modern as British. Mill recognised Hindus as the original inhabitants of this land. However, he did not find them courageous and forward-looking. That was the reason why, he argued, Muslims were able to rule over Hindus. The British in this sequential hierarchy were superior to Muslims and, therefore, they succeeded Muslims and established their dominance over Hindus as well as Muslims. He writes:

> At the time when the nations of Europe opened their communication with India, by the Cape of Good Hope, the people whom we have now described had for a number of ages been subject to a race of foreigners. That subjection, though it had not greatly altered the texture of native society, had introduced new forms into some of the principal departments of state; had given the military command to foreigners; and had mixed with the population a proportion of a people differing from them considerably, in manners, character, and religion. The political state of India, at this time, consisted of a Mahomedan government, supported by a Mahomedan force, over a Hindu population. (Mill, 1826, p. 207)

The existence of 'caste' was projected as one of the main reasons behind Hindu subjugation. It was asserted that since Hindu society was not united and was divided along caste-lines, it could not resist the powerful Muslim invasion that changed the course of Indian history. According to Mill:

> Mahomedans were exempt from the institution of caste; that institution which stands a more effectual barrier against the welfare of human nature than any other institution which the workings of caprice and of selfishness have ever produced. Under the Mahomedan despotisms of the East, nearly as much as in republics themselves, all men are treated as equal. There is no noble, no privileged class. (Mill, 1826, p. 340)

Mill does not stop here. He goes on to describe the temperament and mannerisms of Hindus and Muslims. He writes:

> In point of address and temper, the Mahomedan is less soft, less smooth and winning than the Hindu. Of course he is not so well liked by his lord and master the Englishman; who desires to have nothing more to do with him, than to receive his obedience. In truth, the Hindu, like the Eunuch, excels in the qualities of a slave. The indolence, the security, the pride of the despot, political or domestic, find less to hurt them in the obedience of the Hindu, than in that of almost any other portion of the species. But if less soft, the Mahomedan is more manly, more vigorous. He more nearly resembles our own half-civilized ancestors; who, though more rough, were not more gross; though less supple in

> behaviour, were still more susceptible of increased civilization, than a people in the state of the Hindus. (Mill, 1826, p. 457)

This 'masculine' portrayal of Indian Muslims goes well with the stories of the desecration of Hindu temples by Muslims. Hence, the claim that despite being a minority the Muslims looted and destroyed Hindu temples and converted them into mosques and at the same time, went for forced conversion of Indian society, was a claim that was legitimised. This historical narrative that was the product of Orientalist history, eventually was accepted as an authentic narrative of India's history by the late nineteenth century.[4]

'Nationalist Critique' and the Minority/Majority Framework

It is important to note that the anti-colonial movements of various types questioned this deeply communal imagination of Indian society.[5] It was argued that the British did not want Indians to assert their unique nationalism and hence they had been following a policy of 'divide and rule'. In order to respond to the British argument that the social and religious diversity of India did not allow its people to imagine themselves as a 'nation', the nationalist elites produced an equally powerful idea of 'composite nationalism'.

Three versions of the nationalist critique are relevant for reading this vexed issue of majority and minority in the Indian context.[6] M.K. Gandhi, in his famous text *Hind Swaraj* ([1909]1938) offers

---

[4] For arguments such as these, see Strachey (1894).

[5] For an excellent discussion on the nature of anti-colonial critiques of the colonial minority/majority discourse, see Chatterjee (1994), Pandey (1990).

[6] It would be inappropriate to reduce the critique of colonial imaginations of Indian society to just the ideas of Gandhi, Nehru and Ambedkar. M.A. Jinnah, V. Savarkar—the communists and the socialists—also offered creative and context-specific formulations. We have, however, limited our illustrations to Gandhi, Nehru and Ambedkar to provide a theoretical background to the debates which took place in the postcolonial period. This could be done by using the ideas of Jinnah or Savarkar as well.

a 'cultural' argument, debunking this distinction in favour of the uniqueness of Indian nationalism. Gandhi says:

> The English have taught us that we were not one nation before and that it will require centuries before we become one nation. This is without foundation. We were one nation before they came to India. One thought inspired us. Our mode of life was the same. It was because we were one nation that they were able to establish one kingdom. Subsequently, they divided us.... I do not wish to suggest that because we were one nation we had no differences, but it is submitted that our leading men travelled throughout India either on foot or in bullock-carts. They learned one another's languages and there was no aloofness between them...they saw that India was one undivided land so made by nature. They, therefore, argued that it must be one nation. Arguing thus, they established holy places in various parts of India, and fired the people with an idea of nationality in a manner unknown in other parts of the world. (Gandhi, 1938, p. 42)

The presence of non-Hindus, especially the Muslims, is not entirely seen as a problem in the Gandhian view on India as a nation. He argues:

> India cannot cease to be one nation because people belonging to different religions live in it. The introduction of foreigners does not necessarily destroy the nation; they merge in it. A country is one nation only when such a condition obtains in it. That country must have a faculty for assimilation. India has ever been such a country. In reality there are as many religions as there are individuals; but those who are conscious of the spirit of nationality do not interfere with one another's religion. If they do, they are not fit to be considered a nation. If the Hindus believe that India should be peopled only by Hindus, they are living in dream-land. The Hindus, the Mahomedans, the Parsis and the Christians who have made India their country are fellow-countrymen, and they will have to live in unity, if only for their own interest. In no part of the world are one nationality and one religion synonymous terms; nor has it ever been so in India. (Gandhi, 1938, pp. 44–46)

This explanation should not merely be seen as a critique of the colonial construction of Indian society but also as a contrasting reformulation of the adversarial minority/majority framework offered by Mill. Gandhi does not take us to the realm of factual history or the empirical sociology of numbers to prove his point that Indians of all ethnicities were one nation. Instead, he emphasises on the mutual dependence of individuals as well as communities on each other. This, for him, marked the spirit of nationalism (Sheth, 2018).[7] The question of majority/minority, in his opinion, becomes unimportant if the collective interests are recognised and prioritised. In addition, Gandhi makes a powerful plea to disassociate the living communities from the given ideas of minority/majority. For him, majority/minorities are always constituted contextually. He writes:

> It is a superstition and ungodly thing to believe that an act of a majority binds a minority. Many examples can be given in which acts of majorities will be found to have been wrong and those of minorities to have been right. All reforms owe their origin to the initiation of minorities in opposition to majorities. (Gandhi, 1938, p. 76)

J.L. Nehru proposed the second powerful version of composite nationalism. In his book *The Discovery of India* ([1946]1994) Nehru offered a historically embedded justification for India's unity. Let us quote it at length:

> Some kind of a dream of unity has occupied the mind of India since the dawn of civilization. That unity was not conceived as something imposed from outside, a standardization of externals or even of beliefs. It was something deeper and, within its fold, the widest tolerance of belief and custom was practiced and every variety acknowledged and even encouraged.... At almost any time in recorded history an Indian would have felt more or less at home in any part of India, and would have felt as a stranger and alien in any other country.... Those who professed a religion of non-Indian origin or, coming to India, settled down there, became distinctively Indian in the course of a few generations, such

[7] Elaborating this point, D.L. Sheth writes:

> He found it unnecessary, even undignified, for a people with a long civilizational past to justify their claims to independence on such vacuous terms. Gandhi thus saw historicization of the past as a self-defeating project for Indian nationalism. He sought to revive the old cultural mores but in radically different terms, by emphasizing traditions of co-living of different communities within a political arrangement consented by them. Many political and cultural issues that were pushed into history's lap were brought back into the political arena. (Sheth, 2018, p. 29)

> as Christians, Jews, Parsees, Moslems. Indian converts to some of these religions never ceased to be Indians on account of a change of their faith. They were looked upon in other countries as Indians and foreigners, even though there might have been a community of faith between them. (Nehru, 1994, p. 62)

Unlike Gandhi, Nehru was more interested in producing a historical explanation to justify the nationhood of India. As a result, the time, the recorded periods of history and the space, the known territories of India, become the central components of Nehru's 'unity in diversity' thesis. By this logic, Nehru not merely explains the continuities and specificities of Indian civilisation but also tries to justify the existence of non-Hindu Indians whose religions originated outside the territory of India. This historical emphasis is also used to deconstruct the 'minority problem'. Nehru argues that the minority problem is actually created by the British and the ruling classes so as to maintain their economic and political status quo. He writes:

> Normally speaking, numbers meant the peasantry and the workers, the masses of all religious faiths, who had long been exploited not only by foreign rule but by their own upper classes. Having assured the protection of religion and culture, etc., the major problems that were bound to come up were economic ones which had nothing to do with a person's religion. Class conflicts there might well be but not religious conflicts, except in so far as religion itself represented some vested interest. Nevertheless, people had grown so accustomed to think along lines of religious cleavage, and were continually being encouraged to do so by communal religious organizations and Government action. (Nehru, 1994, p. 383)

Nehru employed this class-based explanation to challenge the British religious frame of two incommensurable religious groups. The cleavage, which did not produce two nations, was of class. He used this reading to criticise the separate electorate introduced by the British in the name of minority safeguards. He asserts:

> Separate electorates for Moslems (and later for other and smaller groups) were introduced and additional seats were given to them

> in excess of their population. But even excess in representation in a popular assembly could not convert a minority into a majority. Indeed, separate electorates made matters a little worse, for the protected group for the majority electorate lost interest in it, and there was little occasion for mutual consideration and adjustment which inevitably takes place in a joint electorate when a candidate has to appeal to every group. (Nehru, 1994, p. 383)

This argument is deeply embedded in Nehru's imagination of democracy and secularism. He does not accept the dominant British minority/majority framework and for that reason found it difficult to recognise the policy of separate electorates workable, even for the benefit of minorities. Instead, Nehru envisaged minority and majority framework as a 'superstructure' problem that would disappear if the 'base'-problem—economic equality and scientific development—was achieved. We shall discuss this point in the next chapter.

B.R. Ambedkar, the third illustration, offered us a theoretically sophisticated and empirically employable critique of the minority/majority framework. He made a distinction between a 'political majority' and a 'communal majority'. In a lecture delivered in 1945, he argued:

> In India, the majority is not a political majority. In India the majority is born; it is not made. That is the difference between a communal majority and a political majority. A political majority is not a fixed or a permanent majority. It is a majority which is always made, unmade and remade. A communal majority is a permanent majority fixed in its attitude. One can destroy it, but one cannot transform it. If there is so much objection to a political majority, how very fatal must be the objection to a communal majority? (Ambedkar, 2014, p. 377)

Ambedkar recognised the fact that the vocabulary of minority and majority had a deep impact on the Indian political discourse. Therefore, he argued for two possible solutions: (a) certain principles should be worked out to address the communal conceptions of minority/majority and (b) these principles must be employed to restructure the institutions in such a way that the framework of communal majority/minority is replaced by the framework of genuine political majority/minority (Ambedkar, 2014, p. 380). Ambedkar's famous memorandum, 'States and Minorities', which he submitted to the Constituent Assembly in 1946, may be described as an outcome of this approach. Ambedkar unpacked the overlapping categories—minority and Scheduled Castes in relation to what he calls caste Hindu majority as follows:

> I interpret … that the Scheduled Castes are more than a minority and that any protection given to the citizens and to the minorities will not be adequate for the Scheduled Castes. In other words it means that their social, economic and educational condition is so much worse than that of the citizens and other minorities that in addition to protection they would get as citizens and as minorities the Scheduled Castes would require special safeguards against the tyranny and discrimination of the majority.… Those who accept my interpretation of the view that the Scheduled Castes are not a minority will, I am sure, agree with me that I am justified in demanding for the Scheduled Castes, all the benefit of the Fundamental Rights of citizens, all the benefit of the Provisions for the Protection of the minorities and in addition special Safeguards. (Ambedkar, 2014, pp. 380–384)[8]

Representation without Democracy

To understand the nationalist critique of the colonial framework of minority/majority, we have to look at the nature of political institutions introduced by the British. The issues of communal/community representation, we must note, had always been linked to the proposal for the inclusion of Indians in the British political system. The representation of Indians at various levels of administration was first introduced by the Council Act of 1861, which was later expanded

[8] It is important to clarify here that in this study we have only limited ourselves to groups/segments of the polity whose distinctiveness is seen primarily in cultural terms. While disadvantage and discrimination show that both economic exclusion and cultural exclusion overlap having a cumulative effect on the marginalised community, and, therefore, Scheduled Castes and Scheduled Tribes also merit the rights argument made here, we have limited ourselves to religious, linguistic and sexual minorities.

in 1892. But the inclusion of natives in the 'responsible government' was contingent upon another equally puzzling question: Who could legitimately be called the 'Indian representative'? By this time, Hindus and Muslims had become two separate groups as well as two distinct political entities in the British imagination. And, by this logic, there was no possibility of having a self-sustaining model of British style representative government in India. In other words, Hindus and Muslims being a 'permanent' majority and minority were not suitable for the rationale of representative government which was, in principle, based on the idea of an 'impermanent' and changing majority/ minority in an elected legislative set-up depending on constellations of interest.[9]

One clarification is needed here. There wasn't any instrumental relationship between census figures of Muslims and Hindus as minority/majority and the effective representation of these segments of the population in legislative bodies and administration. Two 'colonial' arguments are relevant here. First, Indians did not have 'individual rationality', hence, they were not mature enough to run an individual voter-centric modern democracy; and second, India as a political entity was highly diversified, therefore, it could not become a European style 'nationality', and for that matter, a nation-state. In this sense, both Hindus and Muslims as Indians were considered unfit for

---

[9] This contrast between a permanent majority/minority population and an impermanent majority/minority group in government is an important one and merits further study since in cases where the two align, become co-terminus, we will have a situation of minority oppression. It is the fluidity of alliances, based on changing ideas and interests that is the bulwark against the tyranny of the majority because all majorities are impermanent. Alexis deTocqueville alerted us to the consequences of such alignment in a society where there is a permanent majority.

> When an individual or a party is wronged in the United States, to whom can he apply for redress? If to public opinion, public opinion constitutes the majority; if it is to the legislature, it represents the majority and implicitly obeys it; if to the executive power, it is appointed by the majority and serves as a passive tool in its hands. The public force consists of the majority under arms; the jury is the majority invested with the right of hearing judicial cases; and in certain states even judges are elected by the majority. However, iniquitous or absurd the measure of which you complain, you must submit to it as well as you can. (DeTocqueville, 1964, p. 295)

democracy; and even if they were to be given some democratic space in a responsible government, they were certainly not going to utilise it because of their inherent hostility towards each other.[10] However, this did not mean that there were no possibilities to prepare Indians communities for active rational politics. In the first decade of the twentieth century, the colonial state devised a two-fold mechanism to accommodate Indians in legislative bodies.

Separate Electorate, Reservations and Weightage System

In the colonial system, legislative structures were designed in such a way that the interests of various competing groups could be addressed. The introduction of separate electorates for Muslims in 1909 was one such move. The Government of India Acts of 1919 and 1935 extended these provisions to Sikhs, Indian Christians and a host of other communal and occupational groups. In 1925, the colonial government initiated the policy of reserving a certain percentage of direct appointments to government service for Muslims. This was further extended to other communities under the Government of India Act of 1935 (Clokie, 1936).

This notion of separate electorate requires some elaboration here. In the post-1857 period, a strong pro-British Muslim politics evolved, especially after the formation of the Aligarh school in 1875 by Syed Ahmad Khan. These English educated Muslim elite were competing with the English-educated Hindu (especially Bengali) elite. This elite competition became very obvious in 1890s when a revised Council Act was enacted. The Muslim elite made two points. First, in all elections (Legislative Councils or for local bodies) the Muslims must

[10] Partha Chatterjee's conceptualisation of 'rule of colonial difference' is useful here. He argues that in theory, the modern political institutions, introduced by the colonial state itself, were supposed to possess certain universally accepted characteristics. However, in practice, these institutions were seen as external and superior to native sensibilities. Thus, the colony was an exception to the universally accepted principles of these institutions. The impulse to modernise under colonial conditions was to be managed in such a manner that colonial difference could be maintained and reproduced (Chatterjee, 1993, pp. 19–32).

be represented by Muslims; and these Muslim representatives must separately be elected by purely Muslim voters.

Secondly, and perhaps most importantly, it was argued that the Muslim community's representation must be commensurate not merely with their numerical strength, but also with their political importance and with the value of the contribution they made to the defence of the Empire (Coupland, 1944). These two demands became the basis for an important colonial technique, the 'weightage system'. The Muslims were given more seats than they were entitled to by numbers only, and, while voting also in general constituencies side by side with Hindus, they were to vote for their own members in separate and wholly Muslim constituencies. In other words, under the 1909 Act Muslims were given the following rights:

1. Right to elect their representatives
2. Right to elect their representatives by separate electorates,
3. Right to vote in the general electorates as well,
4. Right to weightage in representation.

The provisions were applied to all British Provinces except the Punjab and the Central Provinces (CP). It was not applied to the Punjab province because such special protection was considered unnecessary for the Muslims of Punjab as they were a majority there and it was not applied to the CP because it had no Legislative Council in 1909.

Restricted Voting Right

The colonial state did not expand the scope of voting rights. In the Government of India Act, 1919, for instance, the elected constituencies were classified into 'General Constituencies' and 'Special Constituencies'. The General Constituencies were further divided into Muhammadan, non-Muhammadan, European, non-European and Sikh Constituencies. Interestingly, except religion, the qualifications for being a voter in all general constituencies remained the same, the 'ownership or occupation of a building, assessment or payment of municipal or cantonment rates or taxes, assessment or payment of income tax and the holding of land'. These were the criteria required to enable a male member of a community to be recognised as a voter.

The Indian Franchise Committee Report of 1932 that was set up to map the debate on popular elections and universal adult franchise, categorically argued that:

> In agreement with all local Governments and provincial Committees, the Committee are of opinion that....the introduction of complete adult franchise is impracticable in India.... The Committee recommends that the franchise in all the provinces should be based on the following qualifications: (a) Property … which has been the basis for the franchise hitherto, should be retained as one qualification for the vote, (b) Education … an educational qualification should be introduced which will be independent of property, and which should, so far as possible, be uniform throughout the country. (The Indian Franchise Committee Report, 1932, pp. 175–178)

It shows that the colonial state was hesitant to recognise the idea of popular democracy in India. However, at the same time, it showed great interest in addressing the Hindu–Muslim antagonism with regard to the debate on adequate political representation. This paradoxical equation—representation without democracy—continued to dominate the political discourse in the 1940s. The 'weightage system' was understood either as a reflection of Muslim appeasement or as a recognition of political distinctness as a nation of the Muslims of India. These debates of high politics, quite astonishingly, did not pay attention to the fact that only rich, educated and propertied Hindus and Muslims were entitled to elect the Muslims/Hindus elites as their representatives!

Minority, Second Majority, Nationality and the Law

Two corresponding trajectories, the evolution of British judicial system in India and the emergence of religious reform movements of the nineteenth century, in a significant way, also helped in consolidating the official category of 'minority'. The colonial state recognised the religiously sanctioned norms and customs of each religious community on the lines of the prevalent notion of the customary law. The policy of non-intervention, which the British strictly adhered to, paved the way for a new category of laws called 'personal laws'. The Shariat Application Act, 1937 elaborates this point.

The term *sharia* or Shariat, which became a dominant idiom of Muslim religiosity in colonial/postcolonial India, was legally defined as a collection of codified rules and norms based on the Quran and Hadiths (saying and acts of the Prophet Mohammad). Since this codification has always been subject to various interpretations, there were various shariats among *sunnis* and *shias*—two prominent Islamic sects. However, the idea that the Shariat should be treated as the most authentic set of governing principles for Indo-Islamic communities came into existence only in the eighteenth century. Despite the fact that a large part of the subcontinent was ruled by Muslim kings and rulers before the British the norms to govern political affairs as well as sociocultural life of Muslims were not entirely based on a set of rules and interpretations called *Shariat*. There were many different sources that constituted the religious beliefs and practices of various Islamic communities. These historically evolved religious and cultural practices were termed as 'customary laws', which were separated from 'personal' laws in the later period by the British judiciary.

The translation of the Quran (in Persian and later in Urdu) and circulation of the *Tafseer* literature (books that deal with interpretations of religious texts and offer contextual explanations) established a clear distinction between 'Shariat-based ideal Islam' and the 'customary practices' associated with various Muslim communities in the mid-nineteenth century. The Muslim reformers, particularly the *ulema*, constructed a highly idealised picture of classical Islam and started marking the actual cultural practices as un-Islamic. In fact, the term *gair-Sharai* (anti-Shariat) was established as an explanatory category in religious texts. Since, the Shariat-based Islam had already been recognised by the colonial state, following its policy of non-intervention, customary practices lost their potential as a source of law (Galanter, 1972). The Wakf al-Ulaulad Act, 1913 and the Muslim Personal Law (Shariat) Application Act, 1937, in this sense, evolved out of this legal schema.

One may observe a very similar trajectory among Sikhs in colonial India. The assertion that Sikhs were different from Hindus gradually evolved out of the Sikh reform movements (Fazal, 2015). It was legally consolidated through a series of laws such as the Anand Marriage Act (1909) and the Sikh Gurudwara Reform Act (1925). For instance, the Anand Marriage Act legitimised the marriage between two practicing Sikh individuals performed through the ritual of *Anand Karaj* essentially as a legitimate Sikh marriage. The marital ties between Hindus and Sikhs that were quite frequent in colonial Punjab remained outside the scope of this Act. Section 2 of the Act very clearly stated:

> All marriages which may be or may have been duly solemnised according to the Sikh Marriage ceremony called Anand shall be and shall be deemed to have been with effect from the date of the solemnization of each respectively, good and valid in law. In view of the diversity of our population, rites and customs of marriage vary from community to community. Sometimes doubts might arise as to the validity of certain marriages. The Act seeks to give statutory recognition to a marriage rite of the Sikhs called 'Anand'. (The Anand Marriage Act, 1909)

The Sikh Gurudwara Reform Act (1925) was another legal move to consolidate the Sikh identity as a religious minority. It is worth noting that the Gurudwara reform movement led by the *Akalis* (a term derived from the Sikh scriptures that means 'immortal') aimed at establishing the control over Sikh religious shrines. The Akalis were campaigning against the Mahants—who had traditionally been the custodians of the Gurudwaras. Since these traditional custodians did not subscribe to the Sikhism that believed in Ten Gurus and the Granth Sahib (such as Udasi sect, which claimed to follow the Sikhism of Guru Nanak and did not conform to the Khalsa appearance as ordained by the last Guru), one of the main objectives of the Akali movement was to establish a desired correlation between a tangible, universal and permanent Sikh identity and the functioning of Sikh shrines. This paved the way for the creation of the Shiromani Gurudwara Prabandhak Committee (SGPC)—one of the most powerful Sikh religious institution (Fazal, 2015, pp. 112–113). The definition of a Sikh in legal terms is a good example to underline this reformation of Sikh identity as a distinct religious group.

Section 9 of the 1925 Act notes:

> 'Sikh' means a person who professes the Sikh religion or, in the case of a deceased person, who professed the Sikh religion or was known to be a Sikh during his life time. If any question arises as to whether any living person is or is not a Sikh, he shall be deemed respectively to be or not to be a Sikh according [sic] as he makes or refuses to make in such manner as the … may prescribe the following declaration: *I solemnly affirm that I am a Sikh, that I believe in the Guru Granth Sahib, that I believe in the Ten Gurus and that I have no other religion.* (emphasis added, The Sikh Gurudwara Reform Act, 1925)

The representation of separate set of laws as the most authentic and legally sanctioned codified form of Indian religions acquired a very different political overtone in the late 1930s. For instance, the legalisation of Islamic customs in the form of Shariat law was used very intelligently by the Muslim political elite. In September 1937, M.A. Jinnah proposed to make it compulsory for all Indian Muslims to be governed by Shariat law (Newbigin, 2011). The Muslim leaders of Congress also used this legally sanctioned Shariat law to show Muslim distinctiveness. They conceptualised Shariat law as a 'sacred' doctrine which could not be amended or changed and, precisely for this reason, it had to be protected to ensure religious rights of Muslims in the proposed constitutional framework. The 'religious bond' constituted by Shariat actually turned out to be a reference point for asserting Muslim political homogeneity. Two powerful political speeches made in 1940 are relevant to elaborate this point.

Maulana Abul Kalam Azad, the Congress President, in his 1940s' Presidential address at Ramgarh said:

> The Muslims in India number between 80-90 million. The same types of social or racial divisions, which affect other communities, do not divide them. The powerful bonds of Islamic brother-hood and equality have protected them to a large extent from the weakness that flows from social divisions. It is true that they number only one fourth of the total population; but the question is not one of the population ratio, but of the large numbers and the strength behind them. Can such a vast mass of humanity have any legitimate reason for apprehension that in a free and democratic India, it might be unable to protect its rights and interests? (Noorani, 2003, pp. 63–64)

M.A. Jinnah, the *Quid-e-Azam* (great leader) of Muslim League also made very similar remarks in his Presidential address at Lahore in 1940. He said:

> Musalman are not a minority, as it is commonly known and understood. One has got to look around. Even today, according to the British Map of India, 4 out of 11 provinces, where Muslims dominate more or less, are functioning notwithstanding the decision of the Hindu Congress High Command to non-cooperate and prepare for civil disobedience. Musalmans are a nation according to any definition of a nation, and they must have their homeland, their territory and their state. (Noorani, 2003, p. 57)

Both Jinnah and Azad, despite taking two very different positions, seemed to advance the claim that Muslims should be recognised as a powerful numerical entity. For Azad, the protection of Muslim distinctiveness is only possible in a secular, united India because secular-nationalism ensures the rights of religious minorities. However, for Jinnah, the Muslim right to self-determination is just and legitimate because Muslims as a community constitute a nation in a modern sense. Interestingly, both the arguments have survived: India was partitioned and Muslims of Pakistan eventually became a nationality. A large number of Muslims remained in India as the largest religious minority—what Azad, in later years, described as 'second' majority.[11]

The Partition of India, we must note, could also be seen as an extension of the minority/majority framework. The 'minority provinces' of the British India, where Muslims were in a majority were carved out to establish two permanent majoritarian dominions—India and Pakistan. Interestingly, the Partition could not solve the minority question as it was next to impossible to divide the populations on the basis of religion. More specifically, three political formulations emerged that posed serious intellectual challenges to the newly established Republic of India:

- Minority/Majority are fixed entities; hence they could only be recognised as 'nationalities/second majority'.
- European style nation-state is the only form of institutional apparatus that can solve minority problem of the subcontinent.
- Diversity is a 'political' weakness of the subcontinent. Ethno-religious homogenisation is a natural phenomenon and the Partition has justified it.

---

[11] In his famous book *India Wins Freedom*, Azad argued that partition has reduced the political capacity of Muslims. He writes:

> The only result of the creation of Pakistan was to weaken the position of the Muslims in the subcontinent of India. The 45 million Muslims who have remained in India have been weakened. On the other hand, there is as yet no indication that a strong and efficient government can be established in Pakistan. If one judges the question only from the point of view of the Muslim community, can anybody deny today that Pakistan has been for them a very unfortunate and unhappy development? (Azad, 1988, pp. 247–248)

Chapter 3

Politics of Minority Accommodation in Postcolonial India

The assertion that 'Indian communities constitute a specific form of nationality' continued to function as a powerful political impulse especially after the creation of Pakistan. For Nehru 'unity in diversity' was the way out; for Gandhi 'appreciating and accepting the diversity' was the solution; for Ambedkar, 'annihilation of societal foundationalism' was the response; and for the Communist Party of India (CPI) 'revolutionary nationalisation of diversity' was the ultimate answer. These futuristic resolves stemmed from various political ideological positions. To trace the articulations of these perspectives we shall look at the first watershed moment of independent India, the Constituent Assembly (henceforth CA) where a group of political leaders debated for nearly three years on the provisions of a Constitution that were to govern the independent state.[1]

[1] There is an interesting discussion in recent times about the possibility of an unrepresentative Constituent Assembly—unrepresentative in terms of its constitution and in its not having representatives from all the social groups in proportion to their share in overall population—being able to transcend the segmental and social class interests of the groups from which they come and deliberate on the principles and institutions that were to govern the whole of India, that is, to pursue the universal interest. Today this is considered an impossibility since all articulations are reduced to social positionality, that is, class, social group or gender perspectives of the speaker. Where a person is coming from becomes the analytical response. The CA was regarded as one such unrepresentative assembly. They deliberated on the principles that were to challenge and transform social relations and to regulate societal and political relations in the new nation. Over 70 odd years, the constitutional order that has emerged, based on what the members of the CA produced, is considered as the bedrock of our democracy. We flag this point here because the possibility of cognitive transcendence is often denied by the cognitive reductionism that is dominant today.

Three broad arguments relevant to our discussion can be drawn from these debates.

1. Diversity is a positive virtue primarily because it contributes to the unity and integrity of the country; hence, the institutions created for dealing with diversity must recognise 'unity' as a principle.[2]
2. There are various kinds of differences that make India a diverse country; hence there is a need to classify these forms of diversity and evolve an institutional setup to manage them.
3. Sociological diversity of India symbolises the 'live together' attitude of Indian communities. This tendency is very crucial for nation building and state formation. Hence, institutions must facilitate this process.

In the shadow and embers of a bloody Partition, of death, dislocation and displacement of ethnicities, the relationship between sociocultural fragments and the newly created political entity called the Republic of India was very crucial. The Republic of India is constitutionally defined as a unit that is made up of legally recognised territorial and cultural fragments. The very first article of the Constitution states this: India, that is 'Bharat, shall be a Union of States'.

In order to uphold unity as a fundamental principle for institutional make-up, the Constitution proposes two kinds of mechanisms: (a) the institutions must be created on an overtly secular basis so as to maintain an imaginary dividing line between religion and public institutions; (b) certain specific institutions must be created to address diverse

[2] Rev Jerome D'souza made an interesting point in CA debate. He argued:

> absorption in the sense of cultural or religious absorption is something against which it is necessary for us to guard … the strength of this land will be based upon the strength of individual members of the different communities. And they will not achieve their full strength unless they base themselves on convictions and ideals which are their very own. Cultural autonomy for which I am pleading and which has been promised as far as it is not inconsistent with national strength, even though it may appear in some sense as opposed to national unity, is still consistent with it. (Constituent Assembly Debate [CAD], III, p. 296; quoted in Bajpai, 2000: fn 13)

group interests. These institutions, it is hoped, will help in dissolving centrifugal tendencies and facilitate the participation of communities and groups in the nation-building project.

Undefined 'Minority' and Secular Institutions

The creation of these two kinds of institutions was actually an outcome of interesting discussions in the CA on the very idea of a minority.[3] The idea of a minority in colonial India, as it is well known, was not conceptualised in the standard British political theory tradition. Minority–majority in colonial India was not entirely related to the numerical strength of a group in a legislative body. There were other considerations as well. Minority meant religious groups, depressed classes and tribal communities. The problems associated with the notion of a minority were recognised in the CA, especially after the formation of Pakistan.

On 16 November 1949, a resolution was moved in the CA by T.T. Krishnamachari, that read: 'That in Part XVI of the Constitution, for the word minorities wherever it occurs, the words "certain classes" be substituted.' This suggestion was incorporated in the final draft of the Constitution in a different form. The term 'minority' was not elaborated or defined but it was used as an unspecified expression with regard to the distinctiveness of a group. On the other hand, the Scheduled Castes (SCs) and Scheduled Tribes (STs) as administrative categories were introduced as 'certain classes'. Two key ideas emerged from this distinction, social justice for some groups and cultural distinctiveness for other groups. Provisions of the constitution codify these objectives. In fact, the policies for mainstreaming of SCs largely

[3] We do not overstate the role of Constituent Assembly here. Constitution as a document is a codified form of a political consensus. Aditya Nigam makes a very interesting argument in this regard. Recognising the Constitution as an 'outcome of negotiations that brought forth the "Indian nation"', Nigam describes the CA as the 'intellectual core of the emerging state' (Nigam, 2004).

emerged from the social justice framework while the distinctiveness of tribal cultures was not given adequate attention for a long time.[4]

This legal-constitutional scheme transformed terms such as minority, SCs and STs into secular administrative categories to respond to various forms of sociological and cultural diversity. For instance, if a social group is culturally/religiously/linguistically distinct and numerically inferior, it might be recognised as a 'minority'. If a social group had experienced caste discrimination and/or untouchability in the past it would be included in the 'Scheduled Castes' list. And, indigenous communities or tribes are to be officially recognised as 'Scheduled Tribes'. Since minority, SCs, and STs (and later the Other Backward Classes, the OBCs) are conceived as open, secular, administrative templates, no social group, technically speaking, would become a permanent constituent of these official-secular classifications.

This relative openness of legal-constitutional categories, as we shall see, contributes to the revival, production and reproduction of competing political discourses in different contexts. This revised constitutional interpretation also outlines two features of minority groups: the 'distinctiveness' of minority group in relation to majority culture (Articles 29–30); and the 'diversity' of minorities, which means recognition of various religious as well as linguistic communities as minorities (Articles 25, 26, 350). The first feature very categorically stresses upon the fact that minority being a numerical expression cannot be attributed to any particular social group as an absolute and fixed minority. For instance, Sikhs in India are a religious minority. But, at the same time, they constitute a majority on religious grounds

[4] The Report of the Advisory Committee on Minorities (1947) classified minorities into three groups: A, B and C. Group 'A' consisted of Anglo Indians, Parsees and Plains, Tribesmen in Assam. These groups accounted for less than half per cent of the population. Group B consisted of Indian Christians and Sikhs who accounted for more than half a percent but did not exceed 1.5 per cent. Group 'C' consisted of Muslims and Scheduled Castes who constituted more than 1.5 per cent of the total population (CAD, Vol. 5).

in the state of Punjab. This sociological and spatial dimension makes minority a highly fluid category. The second feature suggests that the multiplicity of identity markers makes the notion of a minority a plural concept. In this sense, the region, language and culture also become significant indicators and aspects to be taken into account to categorise minorities. For example, Hindus constitute a religious majority in the state of Tamil Nadu. However, the Hindi speaking Hindu would be a linguistic minority in the same state as they are numerically inferior to the Tamil speaking Hindus and non-Hindus on linguistic grounds.

These features of the newly created official category called minority did not correspond to the debate on political representation in the 1950s. The demand to provide reservation to religious minorities in the Parliament (and State Assemblies), and in jobs, was rejected by the CA (also discussed in the chapter 'Policy Initiatives for Minorities'). Similarly, the proposal to have proportional representation for minorities was also not accepted. The final draft of the Constitution provided reservation only for the SC and ST groups; while minorities were given 'safeguards' to protect distinctiveness—cultural, religious and educational.

The comment made by Z.H. Lari, a Muslim member, in the CA is very instructive. He argued, 'There should be multi-member constituencies, of say two, three or four to be fixed by Parliament—resulting in allowing the minorities to group their votes'. In order to substantiate this point, Lari further notes:

> on 15 October 1947, the national executive of the Socialist Party adopted a resolution in the course of which it is said, 'All election should be by direct, secret, adult suffrage, under a system of joint electorate. There should be multi-member constituencies, and voting should be according to the system of cumulative votes, thus providing for minority representation.' (Noorani, 2003, p. 86)

The political representation of minorities was also raised by Jayprakash Narayan. He wrote a letter to Nehru describing the possible problems of the proposed Indian electoral system based on the single-member constituency. Narayan was particularly concerned about the 'exclusion of minorities'. He argued that opposition parties had favoured a three-member constituency with a cumulative vote as the first choice and single member constituency as the second (SWJN, Vol. 15, p. 240).

However, Nehru did not accept this proposal. He did not merely defend the single-member constituency as the most effective mode for ensuring democratic participation of people as voters, but also brought in the question of political education. Rejecting the proportional representation system, he said:

> I could understand a complete system of proportional representation by a single transferable vote and plural constituencies. That is physically impossible as it is very intricate... . If we introduced proportional representation that would make it absolutely impossible, both from organizational point of view, and that of the voter who will not understand its intricacies. (SWJN, Vol. 15, p. 240)

There was another rather informal proposal to ensure the representation of minorities in legislative bodies. It was suggested by the Uttar Pradesh (UP) government that 143 two-member constituencies must be created for the state Legislative Assembly consisting of 430 seats. While each of the 90 such constituencies were to have a seat reserved for the SCs, the other 53 constituencies would have unreserved seats to facilitate the return of some Muslims, if possible (SWJN, Vol. 15, p. 240). Nehru opposed this move. He argued:

> I am entirely opposed to any two-member constituency, except where a seat is reserved for the Scheduled Caste or Tribe. I think this will be contrary to the Cabinet decision and, in any event, undesirable. The UP government should be so informed. (SWJN, Vol. 15, p. 240)

Nehru's reluctance to recognise minority representation is important here. He seems to make a clear distinction between the idea of minority representation during British Raj where the minority was a fixed sociological category and the postcolonial constitutional arrangement that conceives of minority as a fluid, impermanent category. In this framework, therefore, citizens belonging to religious minorities are to be treated as rights-bearing members of the state while, at the same time, the state is committed to protect the religious distinctiveness of these citizens when they assert their religious identities of being Muslims, Christians or Sikhs. This relationship between an ideological position, from minorities to citizens and also of citizens as individuals has played out in a very different way in the 70 odd years of the Indian Republic.

Accommodating Minorities: Social Justice versus Right to Religion

An important question arises here: If the rights of the 'minorities' are primarily concerned with the protection of cultural/religious distinctiveness, what are the possible ways by which the socioeconomic and educational backwardness of members of officially recognised minorities groups could be addressed?[5] This question is important because the Constitution makes provisions to identify the backwardness of social groups and encourages the state to design appropriate policies to tackle the same. While the Nehru government of the 1950s also showed a great interest in the issue of socioeconomic backwardness the actual institutional response was at variance with this interest.

The Report of the First Backward Classes Commission, 1955 is a revealing example of this point. The commission, popularly known as the Kaka Kalekar Committee, intended to identify the backwardness of the non-SCs and non-STs Communities. The Commission's response to Muslim backwardness especially in relation to caste-based social stratification among Muslims is very intriguing. The Report notes:

> There were representatives on behalf of some Muslim organizations asking that all Muslims should be treated as backward and be given

[5] This is a question that has a resonance in Europe especially where minorities, particularly of migrants from the ex-colonies of some countries of Europe, remain economically disadvantaged.

> educational aid and adequate representation in government service. It would not be fair, or just, to list all Muslims are socially and educationally backward. *Officially Muslims do not recognize any caste.* It must be said to the credit of Islam that it did not compromise its position in the matter of untouchables ... gradually, however, Islamic society in India succumbed to the influence of caste and lost its pristine purity. The racial distinction of Mughal and Pathan, Shaikh and Syed has been maintained though without any sense of social inferiority. We have recognized this deterioration that has overcome Muslim society today and added the names of such backward communities found among them in list of other backward classes. (emphasis added; The Report of the First Backward Classes Commission, 1953, p. 27)

Despite identifying the internal divisions among Muslims, the report does not give adequate attention to crucial sociological differences in the wider context of affirmative action. It lists the relative marginalisation of those who are socially/culturally treated as inferior in a somehow mechanical manner simply abiding by the Nehruvian policy of non-interference in the affairs of minorities.

The Presidential Order 1950 (that has been amended twice) is another relevant example, which actually restricts the entry of Muslims and Christian castes into the SC list. The Order says: '…the castes, races or tribes or parts of, or groups within, castes or tribes … shall, in relation to the States to which those Parts are respectively related, be deemed to be Scheduled Castes'. However, this general definition of the 'Scheduled Castes' is further clarified. The next paragraph of the Order notes: '*No person who professes a religion different from the Hindu, the Sikh or the Buddhist religion shall be deemed to be a member of a Scheduled Caste*' (emphasis added, NCLRM Report, 2007, p. 139).

Here, it is clear that in order to avail the benefit of reservation, the members of the identified SCs would have to stay within the Hindu-fold.[6] The socially backward Muslims and Christians are not

[6] It is important to note that the Constitutional validity of this Order has been challenged. The Supreme Court has yet to decide this issue. However, in Soosai vs. UOI 1985 (Supp) S.C.C. 590 case, the Supreme Court accepted that the conversion from Hinduism to Christianity did not affect the caste status of a person.

entitled to reservation.[7] In other words, conversion to Christianity and Islam by the 'weaker sections' is officially identified as a serious challenge to the very nature of affirmative action policies.

Article 25(1) Right to Propagate versus Public Order

It is worth noting that there was an extensive discussion in the CA on the question of religious conversion. Despite a range of very strong opinions on this controversial issue, the Assembly agreed to accept religious conversion as an important aspect of freedom of religion. Article 25(1) of the Constitution states: 'Subject to public order, morality and health and to the other provisions of this Part, all persons are equally entitled to freedom of conscience and the right freely to profess, practise and propagate religion'. It is important to mention here that Article 25 is a Fundamental Right, which is justiciable. Hence, the commitment expressed in relation to freedom of religion in this article (and for that matter, propagation of religion) constitutes the 'basic structure' of the Constitution itself.[8]

The word 'propagation', we must note, has been a highly contested issue in the postcolonial legal-constitutional discourse (Sorabjee, 2000). A variety of laws have been legislated to deal with what is often referred to as 'forced conversion'. In fact, 'public order, morality and health' are often given precedence over 'right to profess and propagate

---

[7] It is important to clarify that this religion based restriction is only for the SC category. Muslim and Christian communities can be included into the fold of STs and OBCs.

[8] In the famous Kesavananda Bharati vs. State of Kerala (1973) case the Supreme Court proposed the doctrine of the basic structure of the Indian Constitution, which in any case, cannot be amended or changed by the Parliament. The judgement says: 'The basic structure may be said to consist of the following features: (1) Supremacy of the Constitution; (2) Republican and Democratic form of Government; (3) Secular character of the Constitution; (4) Separation of powers between the Legislature, the Executive and the Judiciary; (5) Federal character of the Constitution. The above structure is built on the basic foundation, i.e., the dignity and freedom of the individual. This is of supreme importance. This cannot by any form of amendment be destroyed' [His Holiness Kesavananda Bharati and Ors. vs. State of Kerala and Anr. (1973) 4 SCC 225]. It is clear from this judgement that freedom of religion is part of the basic structure of the Constitution as a Fundamental Right as well as a symbol of secularism.

religion' in various anti-conversion laws and the court rulings upholding them. States such as Madhya Pradesh, Odisha, Gujarat, Tamil Nadu, Himachal Pradesh and Rajasthan have their separate anti-conversion laws. These laws empower the state to control the activities of those organised religions that use different means (including force) to convert people, especially the weaker sections such as Scheduled Castes (SC), Scheduled Tribes (ST) and women (Jenkins, 2008).

The various official commissions that have been set up by different governments to look at the issue of conversion since independence also make arguments of this kind. The report of the Christian Missionary Activities Enquiry Committee, Madhya Pradesh, 1956 is a good example in this regard.[9] This Committee was set up by the state government to examine the question of forced conversion of aboriginal non-Christians by Christian missionaries in 1954.[10] The Committee submitted its report in 1956 (The Christian Missionary Activities Enquiry Committee Report, Madhya Pradesh, 1956).

The recommendations of this Committee were quite provocative. It strongly suggested that 'those Missionaries whose primary object is

---

[9] The D.P. Wadhwa Commission Report is another example. This Commission was appointed to inquire into the burning alive of the Australian missionary, Graham Staines and his two sons in a remote village of Manoharpur in Keonjhar District in Odisha, in January 1999 (Jenkins, 2008, p. 117).

[10] Explaining the objective and terms of reference, the report notes:

> It was represented to Government from time to time that the conversion of illiterate aboriginals and other backward people was affected by the Christian Missionaries either forcibly or through fraud or temptations of monetary gain and the Government were informed that the feelings of non-Christians were being offended by conversions brought about by such methods. The Christian Missionaries repudiated these allegations before the Government and charged local officials and non-Christians of harassment and as the State Government found that an agitation was growing on either side, it considered it desirable in the public interest to have a thorough enquiry made into the whole question. (Report of the Christian Missionary Activities Enquiry Committee, Madhya Pradesh, 1956)

The Christian community of the state filed a petition in the Nagpur High Court challenging the appointment of this Committee by evoking Article 25. However, the High Court rejected this argument and allowed the Committee to continue its work.

proselytization should be asked to withdraw'. Although a distinction between Indian and foreign missionaries was made and the government was urged to keep a check on 'large influx of foreign Missionaries' in the state, the report conceptualised 'propagation' of all kinds as a problematic aspect of freedom of religion. The Committee noted:

> Any attempt by force or fraud, or threats of illicit means or grants of financial or other aid, or by fraudulent means or promises, or by moral and material assistance, or by taking advantage of any person's inexperience or confidence, or by exploiting any person's necessity, spiritual (mental) weakness or thoughtlessness, or, in general, any attempt or effort (whether successful or not), directly or indirectly to penetrate into the religious conscience of persons (whether of age or underage) of another faith, for the purpose of consciously altering their religious conscience or faith, so as to agree with the ideas or convictions of the proselytizing party should be absolutely prohibited. (The Christian Missionary Activities Enquiry Committee Report, Madhya Pradesh, 1956)

The report, it seems, not merely distinguishes the convert as an 'object' who cannot take independent decisions but also, rather implicitly, evokes an interesting distinction between those religions which could be classified as 'intrinsically Indian' and those minority religions, which are of foreign origin (Jenkins, 2008).[11] In this sense, the nineteenth-century representation of Hindu religion as the most authentic and fundamental religious tradition of India is taken up conceptually to evaluate the notion of religious propagation.[12] Although the report did not describe Christianity as an alien religion directly, the emphasis

[11] Interestingly, the other minority religions (Buddhism, Jainism and Sikhism) were constitutionally recognised as offspring of Hindu religion in this framework. Explanation II for Article 25 says: 'the reference to Hindus shall be construed as including a reference to persons professing the Sikh, Jaina or Buddhist religion, and the reference to Hindu religious institutions shall be construed accordingly' *The Constitution of India* (official e-version).

[12] The Report notes: '... After all, the goodwill of the majority community in any country is the greatest and the safest guarantee for the fulfillment of Constitutional obligations, even more than law courts or executive authorities.'

given to the 'international connection' of Christian missionaries was seen as a problem with regard to national security.

The 'Indian origin of religion' as an explanatory template to evaluate the scope of freedom of religion is also employed by the Indian judiciary on many occasions. Take the famous Rev. Stanislaus vs. State of Madhya Pradesh (1977) case.[13] The Supreme Court had to respond to two questions in this lawsuit: (a) What is the meaning and scope of the word 'propagation'? (b) Can a state legislature (assembly) enact a law that might aim at governing religious issues, as freedom of religion is a fundamental right?

Evoking the Oxford English Dictionary, the Court made a distinction between 'freedom of conscience' and 'right to propagate' religion. It was argued:

> Art 25 (1) guarantees 'freedom of conscience' to every citizen, and not merely to the followers of one particular religion, and that, in turn, postulates that there is no fundamental right to convert another person to one's own religion because if a person purposely undertakes the conversion of another person to his religion, as distinguished from his effort to transmit or spread the tenets of his religion, that would impinge on the 'freedom of conscience' guaranteed to all the citizens of the country alike. (Rev. Stanislaus vs. State of Madhya Pradesh & Ors. on 17 January, 1977, AIR 908, 1977 SCR (2) 611)

The second observation of this judgement was more problematic. It justified the competence of a state legislature (that comes under List II of the Seventh Schedule of the Constitution) to enact such anti-conversion laws as 'forced' conversion might affect public order. The judgement says:

---

[13] This case was about a decade long debate on the validity of two anti-conversion laws: the Madhya Pradesh Dharma Swatantraya Adhiniyam, 1968 and the Orissa Freedom of Religion Act, 1967. The judicial responses in these cases were entirely different. The Madhya Pradesh High Court upheld the validity of the Madhya Pradesh Dharma Swatantraya Adhiniyam, 1968. On the contrary, the Orissa High Court rejected the Orissa Freedom of Religion Act, 1967. The court argued that conversion is a part of the Christian religion; thus, the State Legislature did not have the power to enact the legislation of this kind. The matter finally went to the Supreme Court.

> if an attempt is made to raise communal passions, e.g. on the ground that someone has been 'forcibly' converted to another religion, it would, in all probability, give rise to an apprehension of a breach of the public order, affecting the community at large. The impugned Acts ... are meant to avoid disturbances to the public order by prohibiting conversion from one religion to another in a manner reprehensible to the conscience of the community. The two Acts do not provide for the regulation of religion. (Rev. Stanislaus vs. State of Madhya Pradesh & Ors. on 17 January, 1977, AIR 908, 1977 SCR (2) 611)

This ruling clearly shows that propagation of religion was seen as an act that might disturb public order—partly because it would affect the sentiments of the majority community and partly because the weaker sections of society would become more vulnerable as they lack independent judgement.[14]

The judicial emphasis on conversion of 'weaker sections' is inextricably linked to the modern history of Indian religions that found a very different political manifestation after Partition. The weaker sections—those communities which were considered to be lower in the caste hierarchy as well as tribal communities—were defined essentially as Hindus. In fact, there was a political consensus that the state should play an active role to deal with social problems such as untouchability and Hindu caste-based discrimination through legal intervention. The social stratification in non-Hindu religions, especially among Muslims and Christians, was completely ignored in these discussions. As a result, the identification of backwardness for providing reservation (in jobs, educational institutions as well as reserving seats of parliament and state assemblies) actually emerged as one of the most crucial components of Hindu social reform agenda of the state.

[14] Criticising this judgement, Faizan Mustafa argues that the 'right to propagate one's idea is inherent in the concept of freedom of speech and expression. Hence propagation should also be seen as an expression of freedom of speech' (Mustafa, 2014).

National Integration and/or Minority Distinctiveness

The Nehru government's bold step to amend the Hindu family law was a radical move in the mid-1950s. The government enacted the Hindu code bill but no such legislative initiatives were proposed to reform the Muslim Personal Law.[15] Nehru was severely criticised for encouraging a new form of Muslim appeasement. In the open session of the All India Congress Committee on 11 May 1958, Nehru responded to these criticisms. He said:

> The communalism of the majority is far more dangerous than the communalism of minority because it wears the garb of nationalism. We have thus communalism ingrained in us and it comes out quite quickly at the slightest provocation and even decent people begin to behave like barbarians when this communalism is aroused in them…. (Noorani, 2003, p. 316)

This distinction between minority and majority communalism is important. It underlines Nehru's assertion that the distinctiveness of a minority is a constitutional commitment; hence, institutions should be able to deal with the anxieties and aspirations of minorities, which might take a communal overtone. At the same time, Nehru offered another very important explanation. He sought to clarify the distinction between constitutional adherence to the unity and integrity of the Indian Republic and the notion of Indianisation—an idea that had been propagated by Hindu nationalists, mainly by the Jana Sangh in the 1950s.[16] This clarification had certain institutional

[15] For an elaborated discussion on this debate, see Williams (2006).

[16] The 1951 manifesto of the Jana Sangh says:

> The Jana Sangh considers them (Muslims) flesh of our flesh, the blood of our blood. That is its basic unalterable attitude toward them; the Jana Sangh invites them to accept our hand of brother-hood. It expects them to shed all those complexes which mutilate against this brotherhood. It looks forward to their disassociating foreign ways from the tenets of their religion. They are welcome to worship the Islamic way. They are expected to live the Bharatiya way (see Bhartiya Jana Sangh Party Documents, Vol. 1).

manifestations as well. The Nehru government was keen to establish certain new forms of institutions to implement what was rhetorically known as 'unity in diversity'.[17]

By early 1960s the idea to have a specific institution to deal with the question of national integration emerged as a political necessity[18] that led to the creation of National Integration Council (NIC) in 1961. Though the official and stated objectives for which the NIC was constituted were not entirely related to the problems and anxieties of the religious minorities. The official statement of the NIC, 1961 defines national integration: 'National integration is a psychological and educational process involving the development of a feeling of unity, solidarity and cohesion in the hearts of the people, a sense of common citizenship and a feeling of loyalty to the nation'. Yet, the 'grievances of minority' were given a priority and it was suggested that NIC 'should give early consideration to the setting up of machinery for the examination and redress of grievances of minorities'. It is important to note here that the proceedings of NIC, 1961 as well as agenda items discussed by NIC focused primarily on the problems of integration with regard to linguistic minorities. The issues of religious minorities were discussed under the heading of 'communalism' (NIC, 1961).

---

[17] The University Grants Commission organised a national level seminar in 1958 on national integration. This high-level seminar passed a resolution that was submitted to the government. This was followed by two special meetings of the Chief Ministers that were held in June and August 1960. These initiatives paved the way for the National Integration Conference that was held in September 1961.

[18] In early 1960s, a series of communal riots took place in various states. Muslims, who had already been isolated and marginalised as a religious group by that time, were the main victims of these riots. Although the Muslim League (ML) had lost its organised exclusionary politics in north India, it still had an ideological influence on a local level in UP. In fact, the impact of ML's significant presence in southern Indian states, especially in Hyderabad and Kerala, cannot be ruled out. On the other hand, the Muslim leaders of the Congress were also not very satisfied with the ways in which Muslim identity was ignored in the dominant discourse of development and nation-building. After the death of Azad in 1958, there was no influential Muslim leader in Congress, who could articulate the emerging issues of the Muslims in an acceptable political language. This widespread dissatisfaction led various Muslim ideological forces to come together and think of a political platform to raise Muslim grievance in a collective way.

Non-party Political Organisations of Minorities

This kind of consultative institutional response by the state to deal with the relative marginalisation of minorities also encouraged minority groups to set up similar kind of community institutions. The formation of the All India Muslim Majlis-e-Mushawarat (AIMMM)—an umbrella organisation that was set up by the Muslim Leaders' Consultative Convention held on 8–9 August 1964 in Lucknow was a significant development in this regard. The purpose of the AIMMM was to provide a platform to different Muslim groups and to represent the collective Muslim concerns at the national level. Moreover, the notion of peaceful coexistence of different communities, especially the minorities, was also highlighted by the AIMMM in order to define the Muslim issues as 'secular' national issues. However, despite this unequivocal stand, the AIMMM was seen as a Muslim separatist body in the early 1960s.[19] In the later decades, the scope of the activities of the AIMMM as a Muslim pressure group expanded, especially in the 1980s. The formation of the All India Muslim Personal Law Board (AIMPLB) in 1972 and the coalition of Muslim organisations on Babri Masjid, the Babri Masjid Movement Coordination Committee (BMMCC) in 1987, worked closely with the AIMMM and recognised it as a Muslim representative body (Ahmed, 2014).

The organisations and institutions established by the Christian minority groups are also illustrative of this point. It is worth noting that the Church union movements led to the formation of two main

[19] The organisations like Jamaat-e-Islami, Jamiat Ulema-e-Hind and Nadwa-tul-Uloom and individuals like Dr Syed Mehumud, Maulana Madni, Maulana Nadwi and Maulana Manzoor Nomani played a significant role in the formation of AIMMM. The AIMMM also demanded that Muslim culture and identity should be protected. Interestingly, unlike the 1950, when the Wakf Act, 1954 was seen as a kind of legal assurance by the Muslim leaders, the AIMMM in 1965 asserted that the state should give more powers to the Muslims in the management related issues of Wakf (Shakir, 1972, pp. 57–58). It was a significant change. The 'wakf' properties, particularly in the Punjab region, were occupied by the non-Muslims and the state. Since the government had control over the wakf board, it was demanded that more Muslim members should be nominated to the boards so that it could work for the welfare of Muslims.

bodies—the Church of South India (CSI, formed in 1947) and the Church of North India (CNI, formed in 1965). This process of bodies to represent the Christian community began among the Catholic denomination when in the mid-1940s 'selected delegates of the Catholic Church in India met in Madras to deliberate on some of the challenges they envisaged in the context of the future independence of India' (Abreu, 2009). This led to the formation of the Catholic Bishops' Conference of India (CBCI) in 1944.[20] The organisation finally shifted to New Delhi in 1962.

Responding to the broad idea of national integration from the point of view of the Christian minority, the CBCI made a conscious attempt to carve out an acceptable space for the religious and social affairs of the Christian communities within the constitutionally recognised secular framework. Two broad objectives were outlined in this regard: (a) to promote advocacy on national issues; make representation to Government by liaising with the Central Government and Ministries/ Departments of the Centre; influence government policies for nation-building and development of peoples; and (b) to 'network with other Christian Churches ... organizations ... associations of civil society and people of other religions and all people of good will to work for peace and harmony, for probity in public life, for promotion of human rights and Gospel values' (CBCI website).

The CBCI began to take an assertive role in the later years as a minority pressure group. Two examples are important here. In 1989, the CBCI issued a statement in Shillong arguing for the rights of the Christian minority in general and the new lower caste converts, the 'Dalit Christians', in particular. It is asserted that the Dalit Christians have to face double discrimination. They are unable to avail the benefits given to other SC communities as the Presidential Order, 1950 technically excludes them from the SC category. At the same time, they have not been able to get rid of the derogatory practice of

[20] It is important here to note that the CNI and CSI are Protestant bodies, which were earlier part of the Anglican Church.

Hindu caste system despite being converted to a new religion. The statement notes: 'converts to Catholicism … had hoped for a status of equality, but the structured inequalities practiced in Hinduism continue to be reflected and imposed in the new faith' (CBCI, 2012).

In 2016, CBCI published a comprehensive *Policy on Dalit Empowerment* (2016). An 'Action Plan' was also worked out in this policy document. Apart from recognising untouchability as a sin, the Action Plan strongly advocates for creating a coalition of minority groups. It is asserted that the CBCI will pursue a process of 'advocacy with decision-makers, following up cases filed in the Supreme Court of India and facilitating the struggle to obtain equal rights for Dalit Christians and Dalit Muslims … with faith-based and secular organizations' (CBCI, 2016, p. 25).

The CBCI's categorical response to the controversial statement made by Mohan Bhagwat, the Chief of Hindu rightist organisation, the Rashtriya Swayamsewak Sangh (RSS) on Mother Teresa is the second relevant example. While inaugurating an orphanage on 23 January 2015, Mohan Bhagwat had said that the RSS would not provide the kind of service that was 'rendered by Mother Teresa'. He alleged that the purpose of Mother Teresa was primarily to convert people (*The Indian Express*, 2015).

The CBCI condemned this allegation. In a statement issued the very next day, it strongly argued that Mother Teresa did not follow any hidden agenda nor did she use her organisation for any kind of conversion. The statement also emphasised the national and international awards given to Mother Teresa for her contribution. It is said: 'it is quite unfortunate that the services of such a world-renowned Nobel Prize laureate and Bharat Ratna awardee be dragged into such unwarranted controversies' (CBCI, 2018). Most importantly, the CBCI took up this opportunity to present the contribution of Christian organisations as an example of the *Indian tradition of humanitarian work*. It is argued: 'the CBCI would wish that our nation's age-old passion for truth, unbiased support for the humanitarian works and compassion for the poor and the suffering may not be jeopardized by any cynical motive or intolerant gesticulations' (CBCI, 2015).

The invocation of 'India specific secularism' to defend the rights of religious minorities by the AIMMM and the CBCI, thus, underlines an interesting legal-constitutional form of minority politics. The secularism is not referred here as a division between religion and politics. Instead, the term 'secular' is used by the minority pressure groups to emphasise upon the 'constitutional principles', which govern the discourse of minority rights. This strategic constitutional position allows them to criticise those legislative moves and executive decisions that go against the interests of minorities. At the same time, 'secular' is also employed to highlight the 'political principle of unity in diversity'. The minority organisations work hard for achieving political acceptability as legitimate stakeholders in the public sphere. By emphasising 'unity in diversity' they raise group specific concerns as national issues which are strategically interesting because it broadens the public discourse and compels its adversaries to engage with it.

Language, Religion and Accommodation of Minorities through States' Reorganisation

Unlike the Muslim and Christian consultative minority organisations, which preferred to function as legitimate pressure groups in the 1960s, the Sikh response to national integration was more overtly 'political'. Two crucial developments—the partition of India (which affected the demographic profile of the Sikh community in Punjab in a significant way) and the reorganisation of the Indian states on linguistic basis (which legitimised the demand for an independent Punjabi speaking state) need to be highlighted to understand the shaping of the Sikh minority discourse as a political phenomenon in the first two decades after the independence.

The Partition of India, in an actual territorial sense, was the partition of Punjab and Bengal—the 'minority' dominant provinces of British India. The Sikhs, who were recognised as a minority for the purpose of separate political representation in British India, did not have that privilege after becoming a constitutional minority in the 1950s. On the contrary, Partition affected the population profile of the Sikh community in Punjab in an unprecedented manner. The emigration of Muslims from the Indian side of Punjab and the massive influx of Sikh refugees from Pakistan led to the concentration of Sikh population in a few western districts of the Indian Punjab. This demographic shift had some wider implications. It encouraged the Sikh leaders, especially the Akalis, to argue for an exclusive Sikh majority province within the framework of Indian federalism.

However, it was not an easy task. In the post-Partition India, there was no scope for a religion-based identity politics. Such moves were described as 'communalism' and in the light of the Partition were seen as a threat to Indian integration. Recognising the dominance of this political perspective of the 1960s, the Sikh leadership shifted their strategy to the 'distinctiveness of minority language' as a tool to articulate their political demands (Brass, 1974, pp. 183–185). Hence, the demand for a separate Punjabi speaking province in actual terms was aimed at carving out a Sikh majority state!

This overlap between religion and politics was inextricably linked to the process of reorganisation of the Indian states in the 1950s. The States Reorganization Commission (SRC) was set up in December 1953. One of the main objectives of the SRC was to evolve a procedure for the legitimate territorial restructuring of the country. This proposed procedure was to be based on four identified principles: (i) 'the preservation and strengthening of the unity and security of India; (ii) linguistic and cultural homogeneity; (iii) financial, economic and administrative considerations; and (iv) successful working of the national plan' (States Reorganization Commission, Government of India, 1955, p. 25).

The task of the SRC was, however, highly challenging. Apart from religion, language had emerged as one of the defining features of self-identification of groups in a territorial sense in British India. It was a direct outcome of the process of standardisation of Indian languages that began in the nineteenth century. This standardisation produced an integrated literary form that was employed to underline the distinctiveness of a particular language so that it could easily be distinguished from other languages.[21] Hence, the official languages like Urdu, Hindi, Tamil and Punjabi, etc. defined distinct cultural entities, which were given constitutional status.

The SRC recognised this process of linguistic standardisation by highlighting the inherent problems with 'one language-one state' principle. The Report argues that such a principle 'is neither justified on grounds of linguistic homogeneity, because there can be more than one State speaking the same language without offending the linguistic principle, nor practicable since different language groups … cannot always be consolidated to form distinct linguistic units' (States Reorganization Commission Report, Government of India, 1955, p. 45). That was the reason why the SRC recommends that 'it is neither possible nor desirable to reorganize States on the basis of a single test of either language or culture; a balanced approach, which takes all relevant factors into account, is necessary' (States Reorganization Commission Report, Government of India, 1955, p. 254).

Despite this nuanced recommendation, language emerged as the principal criterion of territorial reshuffling of the country when the States Reorganization Act, 1956 was enacted. As expected, the

---

[21] The SRC also noted this phenomenon:

> The demand for the reorganization of States is often equated with the demand for the formation of linguistic provinces. This is because the movement for redistribution of British Indian provinces was, in a large measure, a direct outcome of the phenomenal development of regional languages in the nineteenth century which led to an emotional integration of different language groups and the development amongst them of a consciousness of being distinct cultural units. When progressive public opinion in India, therefore, crystallized in favor of rationalization of administrative units, the objective was conceived and sought in terms of linguistically homogeneous units. (States Reorganization Commission Report, Government of India, 1955, p. 10)

reorganisation of states on linguistic distinctiveness could not solve the question of linguistic minorities—partly because the boundaries of the states could not align with the multilingual universe of the state population and partly because the issue of linguistic standardisation continued to produce language elites who transformed the question of linguistic difference into a political issue.

The reorganisation of state on linguistic basis in 1956 provided an institutional logic to the demand to have a Sikh majority state in India. It is important to note that the Akali Dal submitted a detailed memorandum to the SRC for demanding a Punjabi speaking state. Four broad arguments were outlined in this regard. First, the creation of Punjabi suba would resolve language controversies and enable the imparting of education in the mother-tongue. Second, the proposed state would be financially viable and empower the state government to use the natural resources in a judicious manner. Third, the creation of such a state would strengthen the defence of the north-western border. Fourth, the Punjabi suba would 'secure for the country a contented Sikh community' (States Reorganization Commission Report, Government of India, 1955, p. 140).

The sequence of these arguments is very interesting. The memorandum seemed to follow the political perspective of the 1960s as well as the principles outlined by the SRC. The demand for a Punjabi state was posed strictly on a linguistic basis. This was followed by an economic argument (that the proposed Punjab would operate within the dominant official discourse of planning and economic progress) and a political argument (the proposed state would help India to defend its borders). The issue of 'religion' came at the last instance—primarily because it went against the post-Partition political wisdom. It cannot be ruled out that there was a political apprehension that if Sikh distinctiveness was asserted without 'Punjabi language' it might weaken the case for a Punjabi state.

These arguments, nevertheless, could not impress the SRC. The Commission categorically argued:

> The case, for a Punjabi-speaking State falls firstly, because it lacks the general support of the people inhabiting the area, and secondly, because it will not eliminate any of the causes of friction from which the demand for a separate Punjabi-speaking State emanates. The proposed State will solve neither the language problem nor the communal problem and, far from removing internal tension, which exists between communal and not linguistic and regional groups, it might further exacerbate the existing feelings. (States Reorganization Commission Report, Government of India, 1955, p. 146)

This official wisdom offered a new lease of life to Sikh minority politics. The struggle for Punjab State intensified in the 1960s. Sikh politics led by the Akalis, under the leadership of Sant Fateh Singh, continued to demand for a Punjabi-speaking state evoking the principles of linguistic distinctiveness of Punjabi. The competitive electoral politics reshaped this discourse in an interesting manner. The post-Nehru Congress found it advantageous to redesign the boundaries of Punjab for maximising political benefits.[22] Finally, as per the Punjab Reorganization Act in 1966, a new Hindi-speaking state, Haryana, was carved out; while the areas where non-Punjabi *Pahari* speaking communities used to live were merged with the state of Himachal Pradesh. Although this move was criticised as a form of Sikh communalism by the Hindu minority elite of undivided Punjab, the emphasis and evocation of language provided political-institutional acceptability to the new state.

The proliferation of the minority organisations such as the AIMMM and the CBCI, on the one hand, and the creation of a Sikh majority state on the other, underline an interesting trajectory of minority discourse. The minority elites overwhelmingly accepted the vocabulary of 'unity in diversity' and 'distinctiveness of language' to carve out a space for minority institutions. The thin dividing line between assertion of 'distinctiveness' (even in a purely democratic sense) and the fear of 'separatism' was always in the foreground of the politics

[22] For an excellent discussion on this point, see Dhillon (1974, pp. 362–373).

of minority demands responding to the official policy discourse.[23] Although the state, through institutions such as the NIC, continued to adhere to the constitutional position on minorities and did not propose to designate any religious or linguistic group as a permanent minority, the idea that the 'minority' could only be understood in religious terms got further consolidated.

Politicisation of Minorities and Hindu Majoritarianism

'Anti-Congressism' emerged as a powerful political idiom in the late 1960s. This political metaphor was mainly evoked to call upon all the non-Congress parties to create a broad electoral coalition. The anti-Congressism, nevertheless, was also envisaged as a social alliance of minorities, OBCs, SCs and STs. These segments of Indian society were considered to be pro-Congress. The opposition parties led by the socialists wanted to reconfigure the social basis of Indian politics and it was inevitable for them, therefore, to propose an alternative political package for these groups.

The rhetoric of anti-Congressism worked very well in the 1967 elections. The Congress lost nearly 60 seats in Lok Sabha (though it

---

[23] The SRC notes:

> It cannot be denied that in a democratic country the wishes of the people of even small areas are entitled to the fullest consideration. But it is equally undeniable that such wishes must be subject to some essential limitations. Thus, for instance, if the principle of self-determination were to govern the internal reorganization of States, there will be no limit to the possible demands for separate States. Every linguistic or other minority group might demand a State for itself, and the wishes of the people could be swayed by purely temporary considerations. The acceptance of such demands would 'lead to the division of the country into a large number of small units. The wishes of the people of different areas as a factor bearing on reorganization have, therefore, to be considered together with other important factors such as the human and material resources of the areas claiming statehood, the wishes of substantial minorities, the essential requirements of the Indian Constitution and the larger national interests. (States Reorganization Commission Report, Government of India, 1955, p. 64)

won 283 seats). It also suffered a major setback in the states. Non-Congress governments were established in Bihar, Kerala, Orissa, Madras, Punjab and West Bengal. This political defeat of the Congress was very symbolic. Although the Congress formed the government at the Centre and Indira Gandhi eventually became the Prime Minister, the social basis of electoral politics began to reconfigure in favour of non-Congress parties. It was clearly reflected in the early years of the 1970s when veteran socialist leader J.P. Narayan began a nation-wide anti-corruption movement. This led to the declaration of national Emergency in 1975 by the Congress government.

In the backdrop of the J.P. movement, an assertive minority politics also began to take shape. The AIMPLB was established in 1972 to assert legal distinctiveness of Shariat. Although the AIMPLB was simply a coalition of various Muslims sects representing different Islamic schools of jurisprudence, who had come together to protect the Shariat application Act, 1937 (a colonial law which ensures that in civil matters, such as marriage, divorce, adoption and distribution of property, Muslim communities be governed by their religious laws), the creation of AIMPLB transformed the Muslim personal law into a political issue (Ahmed, 2018). Around the same time, the Imam of Jama Masjid of Delhi emerged as a key Muslim leader. He started issuing statements in favour of political parties, which were called 'election fatwas' by the media. This 'fatwa politics' was nurtured initially by the Congress and later by the non-Congress opposition parties (Ahmed, 2014).

Around the same time, a new radical Akali politics began to take shape. The Akalis who dominated the SGPC and were at the forefront of the Punjabi Suba movement, continued to question the dominance of the Centre. They evoked the minority rights discourse to represent themselves as custodians of the Punjabi language/Sikh religion. The Anandpur Sahib resolutions of 1973 (later in 1978) were an outcome of this Akali anxiety. The working committee of the Akali Dal in October 1973 adopted the resolution with seven objectives, which aimed to establish the 'pre-eminence of the Khalsa'. The main demands of the Anandpur Sahib Resolution were:

> ... the transfer of the federally administered city of Chandigarh to Punjab; the readjustment of the state boundaries to include certain Sikh majority Punjabi-speaking territory, presently outside but contiguous to Punjab; demand for autonomy to all the states of India with the centre retaining jurisdiction only over external affairs, defence and communications; introduction of land reforms as well as the subsidies and loans for the peasantry as well as the measures to bring about heavy industrialisation in Punjab; the enactment of an all-India Gurudwara Act to bring all the historic gurudwaras under the control of the SGPC; protection for the Sikh minorities living outside the state; reversal of the new recruitment policy of the centre under which the recruitment quota of Sikhs in the armed forces fell from 20 per cent to 2 per cent. (Kumar, 2004)

Institutions to Safeguard Minority Interests

This radical Sikh and Muslim politics amalgamated with anti-Congressism during and after the National Emergency period. In the 1977 elections, the Congress was defeated by the newly established Janata Party and the first non-Congress government at the Centre was established. The Janata Party, which had evoked the 'persecution of minorities' as one of the main political arguments against the Indira Gandhi's Emergency regime, established the National Commission for Minorities (NCM) in 1978. In the official notification, it was noted that:

> Despite the safeguards provided in the Constitution and the laws in force, there persists amongst the minorities a feeling of inequality and discrimination. In order to preserve secular traditions and to promote national integration, the Government of India attaches the highest importance to the enforcement of the safeguards provided for the minorities and is of the firm view that effective institutional arrangements are urgently required for the effective enforcement and implementation of all the safeguards provided for the minorities in the Constitution, in Central and state laws, and in government policies and administrative schemes enunciated from time to time .... The

> Government ... has ... resolved to set up a Minorities Commission to safeguard the interests of minorities whether based on religion or language. (The National Commission for Minorities, 1978)

To make sense of the political significance of this non-statutory entity called National Minorities Commission, one has to understand the technical distinction between the 'statutory bodies' and 'non-statutory' bodies. A 'statutory' body derives its powers from a law passed by the Parliament; while a 'non-statutory' body comes into existence by an executive order. The statutory bodies are also different from 'constitutional bodies' which derive their authority from the Constitution itself.[24]

The Minorities Commission, in this sense, was a non-statutory institution which came into existence through an official notification. It did not have adequate legal weight to respond to the identifiable issues of minorities. Nevertheless, this commission was entrusted with the following functions:

(i) to evaluate the working of the various safeguards provided in the Constitution for the protection of minorities and in the laws passed by the Union and the State Governments;
(ii) to make recommendations with a view to ensure effective implementation and enforcement of all the safeguards and the laws;

[24] These technical distinctions also have some direct political implications. For instance, the 'constitutional bodies' enjoy greater powers and autonomy. These institutions are specified in the Constitution and they cannot be abolished by the government of the day without amending the concerned articles/part of the Constitution. The Union Public Service Commission (UPSC) (Article 315), the Comptroller and Auditor General of India (Article 148), the Election Commission of India (Article 324) and the National Commission for Scheduled Castes (NCSC) and National Commission for Scheduled Tribes (NCST) are examples of the constitutional bodies. Statutory bodies have less authority in this institutional hierarchy. The objectives and powers of a statutory institution are explicitly set out in the concerned legislation. These powers are also subject to subsequent governmental guidance and/or instructions. Most importantly, such bodies can simply be abolished by an act of Parliament with the simple majority. The National Human Rights Commission (NHRC) and the National Commission for Women can be the examples of such bodies. The non-statutory bodies are the most vulnerable of these institutions. They do not have a constitutional existence, nor do they derive legitimacy from any act of the Parliament. The Minority Commission belongs to this group.

(iii) to undertake a review of the implementation of the policies pursued by the Union and the State Governments with respect to the minorities;
(iv) to look into the specific complaints regarding deprivation of rights and safeguards for the minorities;
(v) to conduct studies, research and analyses on the question of avoidance of discrimination against minorities;
(vi) to suggest appropriate legal and welfare measures in respect of any minority;
(vii) to serve as a National Clearance House for information in respect of the conditions of the minorities; and
(viii) to make periodical reports at prescribed intervals to the Government. (Mahmood, 2015, p. 34).

The creation of the Minorities Commission should also be seen in relation to the commissions constituted for the SC and ST. It is worth mentioning that the National Commission for Scheduled Castes (NCSC) and National Commission for the Scheduled Tribes (NCST) were not created as two distinct constitutional bodies. The SC/ST Commission was initially established by the notification of the government in 1978.[25] However, in the course of time, it evolved into a constitutional body. The Minorities Commission had a different trajectory. Despite a number of constitutional interventions, the Minorities Commission could not find a constitutional status during the Janata Party regime. A bill was tabled in the Lok Sabha in 1978 by the government in this regard that could not become a law and lapsed on two different occasions.

---

[25] Article 338 of the Constitution recommends for the appointment of a special office to investigate all matters relating to the safeguards provided for the SC and ST. Following this constitutional provision a Special Officer known as the Commissioner for Scheduled Castes and Scheduled Tribes was appointed in 1950. The growing politicisation of caste paved the way for the demand for a proper commission to look after the issues related to SC and ST. The Janata Party played a pivotal role in establishing the first commission for SC and ST in 1978 as the commission for the SC and ST. In 1987, the commission was renamed as the National Commission for Scheduled Castes and Scheduled Tribes. The 89th Amendment of the Constitution led to the bifurcation the commission into two independent bodies: National Commission for Scheduled Castes and the National Commission for Scheduled Tribes in 2004. Both of these bodies are Constitutional bodies.

The establishment of the Minorities Commission was also a political phenomenon. The opposition for such a body came from two very different ideological spectrums. The Congress opposed it precisely because it was the outcome of the politics of anti-Congressism that was nurtured and practiced successfully by the Janata Party. The Jana Sangh which was also a constituent of the Janata Party was also uncomfortable with it. It was obviously going against the politics of Jana Sangh which had always evoked 'appeasement of minorities' as its core ideological position. L.K. Advani's speech in Parliament in 1992 is a revealing example of this political anxiety. Opposing the National Commission for Minorities Bill, 1992 Advani said:

> I hold myself guilty for having been party to the creation of the Minorities Commission even though on an administrative level without any statutory back up. I was in the Government .... The manifesto of the Janata party issued in 1977 spoke about a Civil Rights Commission, not about a Minorities Commission. That became an aberration, a distortion .... Now this [passing an Act for the Commission in 1992] is being done by the Congress Party .... I am sure that if the BJP had not been there in this strength you would not have been satisfied with this kind of statutory status. It is a relief that you are not able to give a constitutional status .... This kind of Bill is addressed in name of course to the Christians, to the Parsis, to the Sikhs, etc., but actually it is addressed only to one section .... You are going to commit a similar kind of monumental and historical blunder by passing this Bill. (cf. Mahmood, 2015, pp. 71–72)

One can easily point out two kinds of anxieties here: technical and political. The Minorities Commission was just a non-statutory body in 1978 which was to be given a statutory status in 1992. Along with this apparently weak status, it was seen as a problematic institution and was presented as a distortion of the Civil Rights Commission. The political anxieties were more direct. The creation of the Minorities Commission was interpreted as 'political appeasement' of religious minorities in general and Muslims in particular. It is worth noting that the Commission did not make any attempt to 'define' the meaning of the term 'minority'. It relied on an unspecified expression, 'minority', to safeguard the interests of numerically inferior religious and linguistic groups. However, the political class offered concrete meaning to it. The constitutional efforts to disassociate religious categories—Hindu and Muslim—from the legal-constitutional conception of minority were completely disregarded by the political elite. Consequently, 'Hindu majority as victim of appeasement and Muslim/Sikh/Christian minority as victim of communalism' as campaign slogans survived in competitive electoral politics in the post-1980 period.

Protest Politics of Minorities

The success of the Congress in 1980 elections at the Centre, and the disintegration of the Janata Party in a span of three years reshaped the nature of minority politics in the 1980s. Around this time, the Sikh politics in Punjab found a new radical overtone. The politics of Sikh distinctiveness that was clearly manifested in Punjabi Suba movement of the 1960s further intensified and eventually transformed into a new form of political separatism. Some Sikhs asserted that they are a distinct cultural-religious and political group who formed a majority in the state of Punjab and they should have an independent Sikh nation-state called *Khalistan*.[26] To achieve this objective a radical Sikh politics emerged and took a violent form. A number of terrorist events took place in the country, especially in north India.

In 1984, to counter Sikh militancy in the state of Punjab, 'Operation Blue Star', a military operation to retake religious shrines,

[26] Indira Gandhi adopted a highly authoritarian approach after winning the 1980s election. She imposed President Rule in nine states. Punjab was one of them, where the Akali Dal and Janata Party were in power. To weaken the Akali Dal's electoral support, Congress started promoting extremist religious leader Jarnail Singh Bhindranwale. To destabilise the control of the Akalis over Sikh religious bodies, the Congress intervened in SGPC elections and extended support to the extremists, including Bhindranwale's nominees against the Akali Dal. This political recognition helped Bhindranwale to emerge as a powerful independent Sikh leader. In the course of time, Bhindranwale moved away from the Congress. He took a highly radical position. Initially, his politics revolved around the Anandpur Sahib Resolution. However, this extremism grew and led to the demand of Khalistan—an independent Sikh state, in the early 1980s (Jetly, 2008, p. 65).

was launched by Prime Minister Indira Gandhi. The Indian army stormed the holiest Sikh religious place of worship, the Golden Temple at Amritsar, to flush out the terrorists who had occupied it. In the process, they killed many civilians. Although 'Operation Blue Star' was successful in getting armed militants out from the Golden Temple, it had multifarious political outcomes. The anger in the Sikh community, at what was seen as desecration of the Golden Temple, caused the Sikh bodyguards of the Indian Prime Minister Indira Gandhi to assassinate her on 31 October 1984. This resulted in massive communal riots—some would say a pogrom—across the country but mainly in Delhi where more than a thousand people mostly Sikhs were killed. The post-Indira election wave of sympathy caused by the assassination helped the Congress under the leadership of Rajiv Gandhi to register an impressive victory in 1984. Congress contested the election on 491 seats and won 404 seats with a voting percentage of 49.10 per cent.

Around this time, two important political events took place—the Shah Bano controversy and the opening of the Babri Masjid for Hindus. Shah Bano, a 62-year-old Muslim woman and mother of five was divorced by her husband in 1978. She filed a case against her ex-husband for maintenance. In 1985, the Supreme Court ruled in her favour and underlined the need for a common civil law in the country. This judgement created a stir in the country. The AIMPLB and other Muslim organisations launched a nation-wide agitation against the Supreme Court ruling and for the protection of Muslim Personal Law and Shariat. Unnerved by the large protests on the street the Rajiv Gandhi government, in an act of appeasement of the Muslim minority, introduced a bill in the Parliament against this judgement, which later became the Muslim Women (Protection of Rights on Divorce) Act, 1986 (MWPRDA) (DeSouza, 2015). It was seen by progressive groups as a regressive step acceding to the demands of the conservative and orthodox sections of the Muslim community. Concessions were made to patriarchy over the claims of gender justice. This was a landmark moment in the politics of the majority–minority relationship in India where the Congress was accused of pandering to minority elites over the interests of minority women and thereby undermining the secular law that called for equal rights.

The other landmark event in the majority–minority politics of India took place on 2 February 1986 following a verdict of a local court in Faizabad. Based on the Court orders the disputed site of the Babri Masjid was opened for Hindu worship. This was the beginning of a new politics of Hindu victimhood, leading to the growing politics of what has become a category in the public sphere of 'Hindutva'. The BJP (Bharatiya Janata Party, formed in 1980 from the old Jana Sangh and Janata Party) that fought elections on 224 seats in 1984 but won just two seats, found a new lease of life. The Party led a nation-wide campaign to build a Ram temple on the site of Babri Masjid.

The old argument of Jana Sangh that India should become a Hindu nation primarily because it has a Hindu majority was reworked by the BJP in the wake of the Ram temple movement. Echoing the colonial construction of Indian history, it now asserted that Muslims despite being a 'minority' in medieval India ruled over Hindus and humiliated them. They believed that the desecration of Ram temple in Ayodhya to build Babri Masjid by Babar symbolised that historical dishonour. Hindus in independent India, despite being a 'majority', are hence marginalised since they are not given an opportunity to rebuild a Ram temple on the very site of the Babri Masjid because of the politics of Muslim appeasement in the name of minority rights.

The countrywide movement for Ram temple, however, did not provide sufficient electoral support to the BJP in the 1989 elections to form an independent government at the Centre. The Congress managed to secure maximum seats and the Janata Dal and BJP formed the government with the support of the left parties. The short-lived V.P. Singh and Chandrasekhar-led coalition governments in the early 1990s could not stop the BJP to capitalise on the growing radical Hindu politics based on a sense of historical grievance.

As a result, on 6 December 1992, the Babri Masjid was demolished by Kar Sewaks, who were mobilised by the BJP, VHP and other rightist Hindu organisations in Ayodhya. The demolition of the mosque, interestingly, redefined the institutional discourse on minorities in a significant way.

In the backdrop of these political developments, the Minorities Commission as an institution primarily concerned with the affairs of minorities was also transformed. Two important institutional changes are relevant to underline this transformation. As an official entity, the Minorities Commission was attached to the Ministry of Home Affairs since its inception in 1978. However, in 1985 the newly created Ministry of Welfare was given the responsibility of this Commission. This was an important change. For the first time, technically speaking, the marginalisation of minorities was officially understood in term of social backwardness.

The second significant structural change was introduced in 1988. The government decided to amend the 1978 Resolution regarding the creation of the Minorities Commission. The amended notification removed the word 'linguistic minorities' from Para 2 of the 1978 Resolution. The Minorities Commission, which was created to safeguard the interests of all minorities, linguistic as well as religious, eventually became an institution concerned entirely with religious minorities (Mahmood, 2016, p. 39). This official demarcation between linguistic and religious minorities paved the way for an elaborated definition of religious minorities in later years.

Redefining Minorities: Backwardness and 'Minority within Minority'

The institutional apparatus that evolved after 1992 with regard to minorities has three important features: (a) the distinctiveness of minorities is to be understood primarily in relation to the wider agenda of social justice and backwardness; (b) the State officially recognised five religious groups as religious minorities at the national level; (c) the official category called minority was also unpacked and 'minorities within minorities' were also identified and recognised.

In 1992 the National Commission for Minorities Act was passed, which led to the establishment of the NCM in May 1993. The NCM was a statutory body. A Constitution amendment bill was introduced in 2004 to provide a constitutional status to NCM by inserting a new article (viz. Article 340A) in the Constitution. However, like the previous legislative attempts of this kind, this bill could not become a law. Nevertheless, the NCM came up with an interesting notification on 23 October 1993, when the Government of India, notified five religious communities: Muslims, Christians, Sikhs, Buddhists and Zoroastrians (Parsis) as minority communities. This list was amended in 2014 when Jains were also notified as a minority.

The creation of a Ministry of Minority Affairs, which was carved out of the Ministry of Social Justice and Empowerment in 2006, can also be seen as an extension of this kind of institutional response. The Ministry was created 'to ensure a more focused approach towards issues relating to the notified minority communities'. This new institutional structure also responded to the 'internal diversity' of minorities. In fact, an attempt has been made to look at the internal configuration of minorities so as to identify the 'minorities within minorities'. The inclusion of sections of Muslims and Christians in the OBC list is a significant example in this regard.[27]

These institutional changes had far-reaching political implications. The official recognition of minority backwardness was politically employed to demand secularisation of affirmative action policies. For instance, the *Pasmanda Kranti Abhiyan*, a nationwide

[27] The CBCI's documents on Dalit Christians that we discussed in the previous section, also underline the dilemma of 'minorities within minorities'.

campaign launched in 2013, asserted that Para (3) of Constitution (SCs) Order, 1950 should be amended, 'so that Dalit Muslims and Dalit Christians are duly included in the SC list and they are not discriminated against on the basis of religion under Article 341 of the Indian Constitution'. This demand is justified for evolving a more egalitarian politics of identity. It has been argued that

> Muslim politics often talks of electoral alliance between Muslims and Dalits, and/or Muslims and backwards. On the contrary, the Pasmanda politics attempts to create socio-political unity between Dalits and Dalits; between backwards and backwards, irrespective of their religion as Hindus or Muslims.[28]

The most interesting response to the 'internal' diversity of a religious minority has come from the women's groups. The Bharatiya Muslim Mahila Andolan (BMMA), a leading Muslim women's organisation, has been campaigning against the prevalent divorce practices amongst many Muslims communities in India known as 'triple talaq' (uttering of the word talaq by husband three times in one go to divorce his wife) for a long time. Although the BMMA subscribes to the position taken up by the Supreme Court in triple talaq case that this practice must legally be abolished, the organisation finds one universal common civil code (UCC) for all religious groups a politically motivated project. In one of the reports published by the BMMA, it is argued:

> Muslim orthodoxy in India does not want to entertain any talk of personal law reform and the Hindu right is pushing for the Uniform Civil Code … both these sections are coming from extreme points-of-view and both are equally patriarchal. The credentials of both these formations on the question of gender justice and place of women in society are far from impeccable …. There is no clarity about what is meant by Uniform Civil Code in the BJP manifesto of 2014. Are they calling for the abolition of the Hindu Marriage Act, 1955?… On the

[28] A pamphlet published by the *Pasmanda Kranti Abhiyan* in 2013, p. 8.

> other hand, the Muslim conservatives cannot keep their minds and eyes shut to the atrocities such as triple Talaq. (*No More Talaq Talaq Talaq: Muslim Women Call for Ban on an Un-Islamic Practice*, BMMA, 2016, p. 5)

This argument very broadly underlines the 'minority within minority' argument. The BMMA wants gender-just Islamic reforms and they are not reluctant to invite the state to initiate the process; yet, the organisation does not wish to give up the distinctive Muslim identity as a minority in the name of UCC.

The contest between 'undefined minority' and 'defined minority' found an interesting manifestation in relation to the recent debate on citizenship. In July 2016 the government introduced the Citizenship Amendment Bill in the Lok Sabha. The Bill amends the Citizenship Act, 1955 to make the migrants who are Hindus, Sikhs, Buddhists, Jains, Parsis and Christians from Afghanistan, Bangladesh and Pakistan eligible for Indian citizenship as illegal. The statement of the Objective of the Bill says:

> Many persons of Indian origin including persons belonging to ... minority communities from the aforesaid countries have been applying for citizenship under section 5 of the Act, but are unable to produce proof of their Indian origin. Hence, they are forced to apply for citizenship by naturalisation under section 6 of the Act, which, inter alia, prescribes twelve years residency as the qualification for naturalisation in terms of the Third Schedule to the Act. This denies them many opportunities and advantages that may accrue only to the citizens of India, even though they are likely to stay in India permanently. It is proposed to amend the Third Schedule to the Act to make applicants belonging to minority communities from the aforesaid countries eligible for citizenship by naturalisation in seven years instead of the existing twelve years. (The Citizenship Amendment Bill, 2016)

The bill, as it appears, relies heavily on the defined category called religious minority in only three neighbouring countries (Afghanistan, Bangladesh and Pakistan) where Muslims are in a majority. In this sense, the bill seems to underline the argument that the religious configuration of minority-majority in India is inextricably linked to particular countries of South Asia.[29]

This discussion brings us to two fundamental questions:

- Does the act of defining religious minorities at the national level in the post-1992 period symbolise a departure from the established constitutional principle that does not offer any fixed interpretation of the term minority? Or, is it an extension of the principle—an attempt to fill up the emptiness of the official category called minority?
- Minority politics—especially Sikh and Muslim politics—employed two interesting modes to carve out spaces for themselves. During the 1960s minority politics was played out in the name of language (Punjabi Suba, protection of Urdu, etc.) whereas in the 2000s the minority debate shifted to social justice arguments evoking backwardness as a 'criterion' to protect 'distinctiveness'. This shifting character of minority politics makes the question of representation very relevant. In other words, we must ask: What are the emerging forms of minority representation?

Law, Spatial Location, and Minority Rights

The tension between constitutional principles and post-1992 legal developments with regard to defining minorities may further be

[29] This proposed citizenship bill should also be seen in relation to the debate on the National Register of Citizens (NRC). Technically, NRC is the official register containing names of all Indian citizens. The NRC was prepared in 1951 after publication of the first postcolonial Census. It became very relevant in the context of Assam in the post-1986 period when citizenship law was amended to determine the status of migrants in the state (Roy, 2016, pp. 45–51). The process of updating the NRC is based on the revised cut-off date. The names of those persons (or their descendants) who appear in the NRC, 1951, or in any of the official documents up to the midnight of 24 March 1971 which would prove their presence in Assam or in any part of India, are to be recognised as Indian citizens. The draft NCR was published on 30 July 2018 that excluded around 4,00,000 people living in Assam.

unpacked by reinvestigating two technical issues: (a) Who constitutes a minority? and (b) What should be the spatial location of a social group to be considered as a minority? Indian courts have responded to these questions in an elaborate manner. The famous DAV College case of 1971, for instance, very clearly offers us a broad legal principle to recognise a minority.[30] Discussing the interrelationship between Articles 29 and 30 of the Constitution, the Supreme Court conceptualises 'distinctiveness' as the decisive legal criterion. The court observed:

> A reading of these two Articles together would lead us to conclude that a religious or linguistic minority has a right to establish and administer educational institutions of its choice for effectively conserving its distinctive language, script or culture, which right, however, is subject to the regulatory power of the State for maintaining and facilitating the excellence of its standards. This right is further subject to clause (2) of Article 29 which provides that no citizen shall be denied admission into any educational institution which is maintained by the State or receives aid out of State funds, on grounds only of religion, race, caste, language or any of them. While this is so these two articles are not inter-linked nor does it permit of their being always read together. (DAV College Etc vs. State of Punjab & Ors. on 5 May, 1971 AIR 1737, 1971 SCR 688)

The court also discussed the spatial location of a social group to substantiate and concretise its own interpretation of religious and/or linguistic distinctiveness. It is argued:

> Though there was a faint attempt to canvas the position that religious or linguistic minorities should be minorities in relation to the entire

[30] Dayanand Anglo-Vedic (DAV) institutions were used to be administered by the Dayanand Anglo-Vedic College Trust in undivided Punjab. After the reorganisation of the states, the Punjab Legislature passed the Guru Nanak University (Amritsar) Act (1969) establishing a new university. All the colleges located in the territory of Punjab were to be affiliated with this new university. This compulsory affiliation was challenged by the DAV institutions. It was contended that the main object of the 1969 Act was primarily to propagate Sikhism and to promote Punjabi language. It was argued that the compulsory affiliation of the DAV institutions with the new university violated the Article 29(1) and Article 30(1) of the Indian Constitution.

> population of the country, in our view they are to be determined only in relation to the particular legislation which is sought to be impugned, namely that if it is the State legislature these minorities have to be determined in relation to the population of the State.... It is undisputed, and it was also conceded by the State of Punjab, that the Hindus of Punjab are a religious minority in the State though they may not be so in relation to the entire country. (DAV College Etc vs. State of Punjab & Ors. on 5 May, 1971 AIR 1737, 1971 SCR 688)

The observation that a minority should always be recognised at the level of the state has actually evolved into a legal principle in later years. For instance, in the T.M.A. Pai case, the Supreme Court once again asserted that '... with regard to a state law, the unit to determine a religious or linguistic minority can only be the state' (T.M.A. Pai Foundation & Ors vs. State of Karnataka & Ors., 2002). The notification of a few 'national religious minorities' by the Central Government is not seen as a deviation from the established legal principles, especially by the statutory bodies like the NCM. In an official Note to the Ministry of Home and the Nodal Ministry, dated 30 July 1997, the NCM clarifies:

> A national level minority shall have the status of a minority in the entire country irrespective of its local population. This will be so even in a state, region or district where such a minority is factually not a minority in numerical terms. In a particular state, a religious community which is not a national minority recognized by the NCM Act (like the Jews and Bahai) may be recognized as a regional minority. (cf. Mahmood, 2016, pp. 129–130)

This Note also makes another interesting point to justify the government notification of 1992. Evoking the constitutional commitment for affirmative action, it is argued:

> There is thus nothing in the Constitution making it doubtful whether minorities based on religion or language, can be lawfully identified as particular classes of citizens requiring special protections and safeguards. On the contrary, all intrinsic aid to the interpretation of the Constitution, as also the up to date judicial trend, point out that

> religious minorities—like religion based Scheduled Castes—can be treated as specific identities entitled to special protection by the state. (cf. Mahmood, 2016, pp. 129–130)

It is important here to note that this legal interpretation of minority is not exclusively carved out by the NCM. 'Religious minority' as a legitimate category of backwardness at the national level was also recognised by the Supreme Court in the famous Indra Sawhney case of 1992. The court not merely expanded the scope of the term 'reservation' but also made it clear that a religious minority could also be treated as a 'backward class' of citizens. It observed:

> Commission appointed under Article 340 by the President is not to identify Hindu backwards only but the backward class within the territory of India which includes Hindu, Muslim, Sikh or Christian etc. ... the expression is not only backward class but backward class of citizens. And citizens mean all those who are mentioned in Articles 5 and 10 of the Constitution.... The principle of identification has to be of universal application so as to extend to every community. (Indra Sawhney etc. vs. Union of India And Others, Etc. on 16 November, 1992, AIR 1993 SC 477, 1992 Supp 2 SCR 454)

The relationship between 'distinctiveness' and 'backwardness' as two determining principles to define a religious group as a constitutional minority, we must note, is not a fully resolved legal issue. There is a strong possibility that 'distinctiveness' might be understood primarily in terms of the numerical inferiority of a community in a particular geo-cultural context; hence, the spatial location of a group becomes a significant point of reference for the judiciary to identify a minority at the state-level. On the other hand, 'backwardness' is a much broader concept that points towards various national level processes of social exclusions. In this case, 'a community of backward communities' living in different spatial locations may also be interpreted as a minority with reference to national population of different social-religious groups. For example, Muslims in the state of Bihar constitute a distinct religious community; therefore, they are recognised as a state-minority. At the same time, Muslims are also recognised as a national minority by the NCM Act, 1992 as their overall 'development' at the national level has been an important policy concern.

But this kind of straightforward connection between 'distinctiveness' and 'backwardness' cannot be made with regard to other minority groups. In fact, the overlapping of distinctiveness and numerical inferiority is questioned by Rajasthan High Court in the Vijay Shanti Educational Trust case, 2001 (which was mainly about the status of Jains in Rajasthan as a religious minority). In its judgement, the court discussed the NCM Act, 1992 and the Notification issued by the Central government to conclude that the recognition of minority status is an open question. However, the court also pointed out that there was a need to have a legislative initiative in this regard. It stated:

> The question of minority status cannot be decided on the touchstone that any community which has a population less than 50% of the total population of the State is a minority community, the framers of the Constitution may have never thought that such a situation or contingency will arise and the status of minority shall be claimed by followers of different religions and therefore, neither the minority is defined in the Constitution, nor any mode as such has been prescribed to determine as to who should be conferred with the minority status. The rights under Articles 29 and 30 were claimed mostly by Muslims, Christians and Jews, etc., but now such rights are being claimed by followers of other communities also who claim to profess a separate and distinct faith or religion, although they all are essentially and basically Hindus. A stage has been reached when the Legislature will have to think over as to what definite mode or uniform standards have to be prescribed for conferring or giving the minority status and lay down definite norms in this regard. (State of Rajasthan And Ors. vs. Vijay Shanti Educational Trust on 21 September, 2001; Equivalent citations: RLW 2003 (4) Raj 2568)

The backwardness criterion has also been redefined in recent years.[31] The official commissions set up by the government in the 2000s (headed by Justice Rajinder Sachar Commission and the Ranganath

[31] This aspect is elaborated in the next chapter.

Misra) strongly recommended that the concept of 'national minority' should be unpacked so as to qualify the meanings of backwardness of a religious group. Following this principle, it is argued that some sections of minorities, especially Dalit Muslims and Dalit Christians, must also be included in the Scheduled Caste category. In other words, distinctiveness of a religious group is not recognised as a determining factor to treat it as a backward community; instead, a religious minority as a distinctive social group is further divided into sub-groups (such as Dalits and women), who are separated from other members of that group and treated as 'backward'. These policy recommendations have not yet been given any serious legislative considerations in the Parliament so far, even today in 2018. Nor do we have any judicial explanation that can legitimise the claims made by Muslim and Christian Dalits. There are various petitions pending before the Supreme Court and High Courts that question the legal validity of the Presidential (SC) Order, 1950, which we have discussed in the previous sections such as the *Pasmanda Kranti Abhiyan*.

The reservation in minority-run institutions introduces us to another complexity with regard to the overlapping between distinctiveness and backwardness. Two examples are relevant here: the St Stephen's Case of 1992 and the debate on the minority status of Jamia Millia Islamia. In the St Stephen's case, a few basic questions were asked: Is it legitimate for a minority-run institution to reserve seats for its own community? What would be the status of the non-reserved seats in such a scenario? Would the existing reservation policy be applicable in minority run and managed institutions?

The Supreme Court justified the community-based reservation in this case:

> The minorities whether based on religion or language have the right to establish and administer educational institutions of their choice. The administration of educational institutions of their choice means 'management' of the affairs of the institutions. This management must be free from control so that the founder or their nominees can mould the institution as they think fit, and in accordance with their ideas

> of how the interests of the community in general and the institution in particular will be best served.... The minority institution has a distinct identity and the right to administer with the continuance of such identity cannot be denied by coercive action. Any such coercive action would be void being contrary to the constitutional guarantee. (St Stephen's College vs. University of Delhi, 1991 (Writ Petition – civil) 1868 of 1980)

The distinctiveness of a minority as a principle is also evoked in the Jamia case. The Jamia Millia Islamia (university) was established in 1920 by a section of Muslims as a 'nationalist' educational institution. It became a central university in 1988. The university continued to function as a secular institution but its minority character has always been a contested issue. The creation of the National Commission for Minority Educational Institutions (NCMEI) in 2004 gave a new twist to Jamia's minority status debate. The UPA 1 government established the NCMEI to respond to the promises it had made in its manifesto. This specific body was formed primarily to protect the rights of minorities to establish and administer educational institutions of their choice.[32]

The Jamia Teacher's Association and the Jamia Old Boys Association filed petitions in 2006 to NCMEI demanding that at least 50 per cent students from the Muslim Community should be admitted. It was also argued that appropriate action should be taken against the Vice Chancellor and Registrar of the University for non-implementation of the mandate of the Jamia Millia Islamia Society. Responding to these arguments, the NCMEI in its judgement says: '[We] … have no hesitation in holding that the Jamia was founded by the Muslims for the benefit of Muslims and it never lost its identity as a Muslim minority educational institution, hence, Jamia is a minority educational institution' (NCMEI, Case No. 1443 of 2006).

It is obvious from these facts that the minority status of Jamia is a complicated issue. The 1988 Act tells us that Jamia is open to all and it is bound to follow the reservation policy of the government of India.

---

[32] We shall discuss the role and function of this body in the next section.

The NCMEI judgement, however, gives a different interpretation and recognises Jamia as a Muslim minority institution. Since the 93rd Constitutional Amendment Act ensures that the minority institutions are exempted from following the national reservation policy, it becomes possible for Jamia to provide reservation to Muslims.[33]

The Christians in St Stephen's case and Muslims in the Jamia case are interpreted as national minorities by relying entirely on the principle of cultural distinctiveness. It simply means that the principle of backwardness is not considered applicable to the minority-run institutions. In other words, the sub-grouping of national minorities, with regard to socioeconomic backwardness proposed by the Sachar Commission and the Ranganath Misra Commission is not taken into consideration. This poses an apparent contradiction. On the one hand, there is a demand to expand the scope of the Scheduled Caste category so that Muslims and Christian Dalits may get the benefit of reservation. On the other hand, there is no reservation for Muslims Dalits and Christian Dalits in the Muslim and Christian 'minority' run institutions such as Jamia and St Stephen's today in 2019 although there was reservation in St Stephen's from 2008 till 2011.[34] It is apparent that defining a religious minority at the national level is an unsettled issue. The judiciary as well the Parliament must have to offer a solution to the tension between the principle of distinctiveness and the principle of backwardness.

---

[33] The 93rd Amendment Act inserted a new clause in the Article 15(2) of the Constitution. It says:

> Nothing in this article or in sub-clause (g) of clause (1) of article 19 shall prevent the State from making any special provision, by law, for the advancement of any socially and educationally backward classes of citizens or for the Scheduled Castes or the Scheduled Tribes in so far as such special provisions relate to their admission to educational institutions including private educational institutions, whether aided or unaided by the State, other than the minority educational institutions referred to in clause (1) of article 30.

[34] St Stephen's experimented with quotas for Dalit Christian students in 2008. There was a huge public outcry from elitist alumni but the college persisted. The policy had to be changed in 2011 when the number of applicants did not merit its continuance (Chopra, 2011; Guha, 2018).

Formal and Informal Forms of Minority Representation

This brings us to our second broad observation: The nature of minority politics and the question of political representation. It is important to point out that the representation of minorities in legislative bodies is often analyzed primarily with reference to Muslims representation in the Lok Sabha or the state assemblies. This interpretation of minority representation can be regarded as being deficient for two reasons. One, this kind of generalisation does not allow us to examine the difference between the colonial forms of political representation and the postcolonial legal-constitutional specificities. As a result, the minority question turns into a Muslim question!

Second, the political representation is always understood with regard to the Lok Sabha and State assemblies where direct elections are held. It is argued that political parties do not give tickets to minorities to contest elections and hence they do not get effective as well as adequate political representation. This overemphasis on 'ticket distribution' and apathetic attitude of political parties fails to capture the relationship between minority communities (read religious minorities) and their political processes.

Let us take the representation of Muslims to elaborate this point. The dominant debate on Muslim political representation, as it is well known, is all about the decreasing number of Muslim MLAs and MPs in the second decade of this century. It is assumed that if an opportunity is given, the Muslims voters would eventually vote for a Muslim candidate and the region, caste, class, gender and party affiliation would not affect their electoral choices. This imaginary correlation between Muslim voters and elected MLAs and MPs is entirely incorrect. The shrinking presence of Muslim legislative members in assemblies and Parliament does not reflect the nature of Muslim political participation. For instance, there are only 23 Muslims MPs in the present 2014 Lok Sabha, which is the lowest

Muslim representation in the House since 1952 (Table 3.1). But it does not mean that this 'lack of adequate numbers' determines the Muslim participation in politics.

Table 3.1: Muslim Representation in the Lok Sabha (1952–2014)

No.	*Year*	*Total Elected Members*	*Muslims Elected*
I	1952	489	21
II	1957	494	24
III	1962	494	23
IV	1967	520	29
V	1971	518	30
VI	1977	542	34[d]
VII	1980	529[a]	49[d]
VIII	1984	542	46[d]
IX	1989	529[b]	33
X	1991	534[c]	28
XI	1996	543	28
XII	1998	543	29
XIII	1999	543	32
XIV	2004	543	36
XV	2009	543	30
XVI	2014	543	23

Notes:
[a] Elections were not held in Assam (12) and Meghalaya (1).
[b] Elections were not held in Assam (14).
[c] Elections were not held in J&K (6) and countermanded in two seats in Bihar and one in UP.
[d] Including Muslims elected in by-elections.
Source: Compiled by the authors.

To understand the nature of minority representation, therefore, it is very important to look at the other modes in which the concerns of Muslims have been articulated. The Muzaffarnagar riot of September 2013—in which more than 50 Muslims were killed and around 50,000 got displaced—is a good example to demonstrate this point. At the time of riots, the Congress led-UPA was in power at the Centre and there was a majority government led by the Samajwadi Party (SP) in the state. There were total 64 Muslim MLAs in the Vidhan Sabha (State Legislative Assembly) out of which 40 belonged to the SP.[35] This powerful Muslim presence in the assembly (which is almost 15 per cent) is not at all insignificant if we compare it with the share of Muslims (19 per cent as per Census 2011) in the overall population of the state.

The political configuration in Muzaffarnagar in terms of Muslim legislative presence also reflects a very similar pattern. The district was represented by two Muslim MLAs, one Muslim MP and two MLAs from non-BJP parties. These MLAs had won the 2012 assembly elections very comfortably. The Election Commission statistics show that all of them secured more than 30 per cent votes in their respective constituencies. If this is the case, then the question arises: Why did these elected representatives fail to act effectively during and after the 2013 anti-Muslim riots? The argument that if Muslims are represented by Muslims, the magnitude of targeted violence against them would decrease simply cannot be substantiated in this case. This failure of political 'efficacy' points towards the structural logic of representation in the India context. The representation of Muslims, therefore, needs to be unpacked at least in two ways: 'formal' form of representation and an 'informal' form of representation.

The elected Muslim representatives—MLAs and MPs—who may or may not be elected exclusively by Muslim electorates characterise the formal form of representation. This form corresponds to the constitutional principle that electorates residing in a territorially defined constituency constitute a homogeneous community (of voters), whose political interests are identical and, therefore, it should be represented by its own member(s) (Ahmed, 2016). Unlike the formal electoral representation, the 'informal representation' was not dependent on the participation of common Muslims (and non-Muslims)

[35] It does not mean that the SP was the only party that provided an opportunity to Muslims to fight the election on its tickets; there were Muslim MLAs from BSP, Congress and the Peace Party.

as voters. In this case, the 'representativeness' is evaluated differently: influential individuals and religious, civic and cultural organisations recognised as stakeholders to reach out to the concerned Muslim community.

In the case of Muzaffarnagar, the 'formal form of representation' could not work for two possible reasons. First, the compulsions of competitive politics (party line, etc.) could not allow the Muslim MLAs to act exclusively as 'Muslim representatives'. The Second and perhaps the most important point, the elected Muslim representatives did not evoke any grand imagination of Muslim-hood. They responded to their immediate constituency—the community of Muslims they identify themselves with. In other words, the Muslim heterogeneity in UP prevailed over the imposed Muslim homogeneity.

But, at the same time, the 'informal form of representation' functioned differently. The Muslim social-religious organisations—particularly the Jamiat Ulema-e-Hind (JUH)—emerged as a legitimate stakeholder in post-riots reconstruction work. Immediately after the riots, the JUH organised a number of relief camps for affected Muslim families. The organisation also went for a massive national and international funding drive. It approached the UK-based Islamic charity, the Indian Muslim Federation, to purchase a piece of land. This land was redeveloped with the help of local Muslims to construct low-cost houses for riot victims. The JUH then donated these plots/partially constructed houses to victims. However, this was not a pure donation; the owners of these houses were asked to repay the part of the cost of these houses in interest-free instalments (Ahmed, 2019). This neighbourhood is now known as the *Fida-e-Millant Nagar*.

The 'informal' support received by the JUH in rehabilitating the riot-affected Muslim families shows that such religious-civic organisations also function as a representative.[36] This kind of

[36] The India Exclusion Report, 2015 also underlines the inability of civil society organisations to make effective intervention in the post-riot scenario (Hassan, 2016).

'informal form of representation' operates at the bottom level of the society and often receives a favourable state recognition. In a broader sense, it may be argued that this informal form of representation of minorities through civic and religious organisations is not an anti-thesis to the formal form of political representation. Instead, this form of representation is deeply embedded in the collective/ community right given to the minorities in the Constitution.

This brief story of the politics of minority accommodation in postcolonial India introduces us to four different political trajectories. First, the complex relationship between institutions and politics remains a decisive factor that shapes and nurtures the minority discourse. The realisation that there should be a clear distinction between contextually constituted political minorities and the fixed census categories such as Hindu, Muslim and Sikh, etc. forced the political elites of the 1950s to evolve a well thought out constitutional position. The two constitutional principles: (a) minorities should always be defined on a contextual basis and (b) the criterion for the identification of a minority should remain open and ever-evolving, paved the way for the evolution of a specific conception of 'secular' politics. Instead of invoking the conventional understanding that secularism is all about a division between religion and politics, the political elites presented the 'secular' as a template for political accommodation of diversity. However, this positive refashioning of the constitutional principles found a very different overtone in the realm of competitive electoral politics. Although the political elite started addressing the electorates as minority and majority, the actual expressions were never delinked from the established colonial idioms of politics: Hindus as majority and Muslims/Sikhs/Christians as minority. As a result, sociological categories—religion, caste and language—strengthened as the markers of self-identification in political terms. The evolution of the Minorities Commission into the NCM particularly with a defined conception of minorities is an example of this tussle between constitutional principles and political requirements.

Second, the assertion of 'minorities within a minority' underlines another aspect of the minority politics in India. The marginalised groups within the minorities, especially the religious minorities, have to survive in a hostile anti-minority environment. At the same time, the minority elite do not allow these groups to question the internal hierarchies and power structure. They are left with three options. First, they are advised by the community elite to not ask for internal reforms as it would affect the collective strength of the community as a homogeneous entity. Second, they are asked by the orthodox secularists to get rid of their communal belongings and assert their legal identity as a secular citizen. The third option is given by the rightist majority elites, who try to appropriate the internal discontents among minorities to nurture 'one religion, one nation, one country' framework. Interestingly, the gender and caste minorities within religious minority communities in India have come up with a nuanced position. They have refused to give up their religious identities by proposing democratic and egalitarian interpretations of religious texts and traditions and at the same time, they invoke constitutional principles and values to argue for gender justice and affirmative action for backward sub-groups.

Third, the overlapping between distinctiveness of language/religion and backwardness of religious communities has been a very significant political issue for minorities in India. The minority elite emphasised upon the distinctiveness of language—for instance, Punjabi and Urdu—to carve out a space for religion-based politics in the early decades. In later years, however, a new form of politics began to take shape. The political correctness of the 1990s allowed the minority elites—especially the Muslim and Christian leaders—to assert the marginalisation and backwardness of their communities in a more direct fashion. However, this fixity of minority backwardness also had a very different political outcome. The move to declare five religious communities as national minorities, in a way, also strengthened the already worked out imagination of 'Hindu majority'. It had now become easier for the Hindu essentialists to argue that the minorities, especially Muslims, are appeased and pampered at the national level. This argument evolved in political rhetoric in the mid-1990s to underline Hindu subjugation.

The UPA regime initiated an interesting 'academic politics of minority'. This politics had two very clear facets—it was primarily concerned with appointing various study-based commissions and at the same time, it aimed at deconstructing the minority category. The manner in which Muslims are differentiated from other minority religious groups in the post-2000 period, especially after the publication of Sachar Report, is a revealing example of this politics. No doubt that the Sachar Report was successful in legitimising Muslim backwardness as a political issue but schemes that flowed from the recommendations of the report do not seem to have made much impact on the lives of Muslims (as revealed by the Post-Sachar Evaluation Report 2014; also see the chapter 'Policy Initiatives for Minorities'). Yet, Sachar Report emerged as a symbol of Muslim appeasement. The BJP appropriated it to produce a powerful narrative of equality-based affirmative action. The slogan *Sab Ka Sath Sab Ka Vikas* is often presented as 'development of all and appeasement of none'. In fact, Muslim appeasement has now become the dominant narrative of Indian politics.

Finally, the minority discourse in India has produced a very different form of political representation. The Indian constitutional democracy which adopted the parliamentary form of government based on the 'first past the post system' does not recognise proportional representation for any kind of minority. However, the demographic profile of minority groups in certain parts of India (for example, Sikhs in Punjab, Christians in Nagaland and Muslims in Jammu and

Kashmir constitute a majority) affect the logic of representation in a significant way. These groups are able to achieve adequate formal political representation in state assemblies in these regions, but their political presence at the national level remains a highly debatable issue, particularly with regard to Muslims. This political unevenness (political majority at the state level despite being a national minority) has produced a particular kind of politics of 'distrust'. Minority-ruled border states (Kashmir, Punjab and Nagaland) are always seen as problematic spaces, where democratic politics is pitted against the concerns of national security. However, there is another form of minority representation. The community organisations, NGOs and self-help groups run by the minority communities that function as a link between the state and various segments of minority communities. This kind of 'informal form of representation' of minorities actually complements a more direct form of political representation.

Chapter 4

Policy Initiatives for Minorities

From the discussion in the previous chapters about the institutional architecture of the Indian state, where the issue of minority claims and contestations was analysed, we shall now, in this chapter, shift the focus to our third axis of the minority question in a democracy and look at specific policies formulated by the state during the past seventy years. We see that these policies are a response to claims belonging to both the camps—cultural distinctness and social justice and equity.

In most pluralistic societies the issues concerning minorities—ethnic, linguistic, religious or sexual—are not only too many but are also anchored in multiple and overlapping dimensions thereby making the policy templates for minorities quite complicated. At one level there are issues that concern or affect the members of minority groups only. These issues may include but are not limited to the followings: (a) public recognition of language, symbols, icons, festivals and other cultural practices of minority groups; (b) allowing time off work for worship or making an exemption for a dress code, if any, at workplace or in an educational institution; (c) state support for the establishment of places of worship, cemeteries and funeral rites and granting permission to aid and create minority institutions and organisations of various kinds; and finally (d) the desire for maintaining some degree of autonomy in their own affairs.

At another level, there may be issues that are not specifically linked to members of minority groups but also concern members of the wider society. These issues may include: (a) protection from discrimination in various public spaces such as the labour market, educational institutions and political bodies and also protection from organised violence; and (b) lack of, what Gewirth (1996) calls, 'generic conditions of agency' or the ability to convert opportunity into asset; or developmental deficits such as lack of access to basic amenities or to a range of publicly provided goods and services.

Thus, the issues characteristic of minorities are not only rooted in a complex mix of social, cultural, economic and political dimensions but also vary in terms of the policy priority that they may require and the ethical, legal and political ramifications that they may entail. This is seen with respect to both the vertical relationship between the members of minorities and the state and the horizontal relationships amongst the members of different groups.

Given this diversity, the policy response may take many forms and may encapsulate a combination of divergent approaches and strategies. For instance, at one level, addressing some issues may require a group-based approach whereas, at another level, it may be tackled through an individual mode of inclusive policies. Again, at one level, some issues may be addressed simply by a conscious effort of the state and its myriad agencies whereas, at another level, it would be only possible through legislative, legal or quasi-legal backing. In some cases, addressing some issues may require a long term commitment and an institutionalised policy framework whereas others could be sufficiently dealt with through short term and 'ad hoc' policies, based on 'as' and 'when' required.

It is, therefore, not surprising to find a range of positions on and policy frameworks for minorities across pluralistic or multicultural societies. In the Indian context, as discussed in the previous chapters, the Indian constitution clearly specifies the rights granted to the religious minorities. While the constellation of these rights has formed the bedrock of the policy framework of the Indian state for religious minorities, it has never been static or fixed. The policy framework as well as the catalogue of state interventions for minorities have evolved and been shaped over time through many claims and contestations and also, as we shall see, in response to political expediency and the changing public mood in the country.

The ensuing analysis is an attempt to assess India's public policies aimed at addressing issues pertaining to religious minorities. To this end, we focus on four policy realms: '(a) cultural policies, (b) educational policies, (c) social justice policies, and (d) affirmative action and/or empowerment policies.' Of course, these policy realms are neither neatly delineated nor all-inclusive. Nevertheless, we believe that all of them taken together cover a lot of ground.

Cultural Policies

In a democratic polity built on, and characterised by, a multitude of ethnic and religious groups with distinctive cultures the question of how cultural traditions and practices of minority groups get featured, accommodated and represented in public as well as symbolic spaces assumes immense significance. As pointed out earlier, modern nation-states have tended to deal with minority issues variously—from genocide to a demand for integration and assimilation; from mere tolerance to the accommodation of minority cultural values, traditions and sensibilities. Even though many democratic nations characterised by cultural diversity have come a long way to celebrate 'multiculturalism' or are sensitive to cultural sensibilities of minorities, the cultural policies of the state tend to disadvantage the minorities. Across a range of countries, it has been observed that policies pertaining to the declaration of holidays, the naming of places, the permitted religious/cultural rituals that get incorporated into state ceremonies blur the distinction between group cultural practice and national culture. More often than not, on issues such as the language of instruction and the curriculum design in educational institutions the majority community is favoured to the disadvantage of minority communities (Mahajan, 1999).

In the early years of independence, there was a wide consensus among the makers of Indian republic over the idea of 'unity in diversity'. This was a vision that sought to make a 'nation' based on principles of equality and justice out of a heterogeneous population marked by racial, religious, language and cultural distinctions (Vatsyayan, 1972). Even in the hour of uncertainty, anxiety and euphoria that was apparent at the end of colonial rule the leaders such as Jawaharlal Nehru—the first Prime Minister of independent India—held the view that they (minorities) should be given the fullest assurance of their culture and tradition (Gopal, 1988). M.K. Gandhi—revered as the 'father of the nation'—sought to pursue an inclusive strategy by seeking to incorporate religious symbols relevant to Islam in his public rituals, Islamic linguistic forms in his definition of a national language and Muslim political interests in his coalitions (Rudolph and Rudolph, 1987; Sheth, 2018). Eventually, as pointed out in previous chapters, a cultural safeguard to minorities was guaranteed in the Constitution itself. However, there remain vast spaces where inclusion and incorporation of minority cultural specificities require a conscious effort by the state.

How far has India's cultural policy, therefore, taken care of cultural symbols, icons and sensibilities of religious minorities? While an examination of all kinds of public, symbolic and cultural spaces is beyond the scope of this study, we have nevertheless, in this section, considered some important sites and opportunities which are not only critically important for minority cultures to sustain themselves but also reflective of the nation's commitment, or lack of it, to give due representation or visibility to minority cultural icons, symbols, values and practices in its sociocultural life. These include public holidays, naming of street/roads and financial support for religious/cultural activities.

Public Holidays

In modern societies, public holidays[1] are marked as important events. Whether secular or religious, public holidays entail both societal and

[1] The American Heritage Dictionary (1996) defines holidays as days on which custom or the law dictates a halting of general business activity to commemorate or celebrate a particular event.

political meanings and significance.[2] However, in societies internally divided along ethnic or religious lines public holidays may also be seen or taken as an indicator of the nation's treatment to, and respect for minorities. Official recognition and celebration of festivals associated with minorities is not only symbolic to, and reflective of, communitarian sensibilities of the state but also bears great practical significance for the state and for the minorities themselves (Kymlicka, 2008b).

India has a long list of public holidays.[3] As is the case around the world, most of these holidays are associated with one or another religion, and hence are 'holy days'. For instance, the central list of holidays includes about 18 gazetted holidays along with a number of restricted holidays (more than twice the number of gazetted holidays). Of the 18 holidays, as many as 15 belong to the religious/cultural category and include birth anniversaries of religious figures and festivals belonging to different religions. Interestingly, nine of the 15 such holidays pertain to minority religious communities.[4] It is important to note that listing them as national holidays is a deliberate attempt by the secular state to educate its citizens into

---

[2] In almost all countries most of the public holidays are actually 'holy days' marked by specific or elaborate religious rituals. The celebration of these holidays offers an opportunity for those who participate in them to recommit to shared values, beliefs and institutions of their respective communities. And yet, even as these holidays may be associated with particular groups many of these holidays, if not all, also play important role in promoting and strengthening civic integration, goodwill and the sense of harmonious co-existence (Etzioni, 2000).

[3] It may be mentioned that in India there are two overlapping lists of holidays—one framed by the central/national government and the other by the state governments. The holidays declared by the national or central government apply all over the country. However, keeping in view the large cultural diversity across states, the state governments are allowed to prepare their own list of holidays which include holidays other than those listed by the national government. The state-specific holidays are observed within the boundaries of the respective state.

[4] These holidays include the following: Buddha Purnima (Buddhism), Mahavir Jayanti (Jainism), Guru Nanak Jayanti (Sikhism), Christmas Day and Good Friday (Christianity) and Milad-un-nabi (birth anniversary of Prophet Mohammad PBUH), Idul-Fitr, Id-ul-Zuha, Muharram (Islam).

accepting that these days are the days that belong to the whole nation and not just to a particular community. It is the political message of a modern plural democracy aimed at saying that the whole nation must know the significance of the holiday although a particular community may, because of its specific meaning for them, commemorate or celebrate it with special ceremonies. The issue is, therefore, not about religious holidays but about national holidays (DeSouza, 2018a, p. 338).

Observing 'Sunday' as a weekly off day or a holiday in India marks an important element of the cultural policies of the country. On this day, public institutions and offices remain closed across the length and breadth of the country. The weekly off day such as 'Sunday' in the West, and 'Friday' in many Islamic countries of West Asia is seen to conform to the religious tradition and practice of the majority communities, and hence often regarded as being disadvantageous to minority communities. But in spite of the fact that 'Sunday' as a public holiday was introduced by the British colonial regime and has its roots in the Christian tradition, the Indian state after independence chose not to do away with it. Thus, 'Sunday' as a weekly off day in India, in marked contrast to the West, is not linked to the religious tradition of the majority community. Nor is it a site through which cultural traditions, values and practices of the majority community are reinforced. Curiously enough, the practice continues untrammeled, without being rancorous, in spite of rising influence of the cultural nationalists and right-wing political formations.

Even as Sunday as the weekly holiday is observed nationally and yet it is not something cast in stone, and hence not non-negotiable. In many cases, local circumstances weigh in to have weekly holiday suitably modified or altered. It has long been a practice of allowing some public offices and institutions, especially schools, to remain off on Friday instead of Sunday in some areas with sizeable Muslim population. On public demand, local authorities make this particular arrangement so that Muslims are able to offer Friday mass prayer without being at a loss for anything.[5] Such special considerations are again a great accommodative gesture, reflecting communitarian sensibilities of the state.

There have, however, been instances of the insensitivity of the Indian state to minority cultural feelings. The recent controversy over the central government's decision to hold 'Good Governance Day'[6] on 'Christmas Day' is a case in point. This created a furore and was widely criticised. The objection was about observing and celebrating Good Governance Day on Christmas Day (an important religious festival of the Christians) more so because of the conflicting nature of the two. Good Governance can only be celebrated if it is a working day, whereas Christmas was and has always been a public and a national holiday all over the country.[7]

Of late, particularly since 2014,[8] attempts are underway, or already made, to cut down on the number of holidays and to alter the weekly holiday pattern being observed in minority educational institutions receiving government aid. For instance, the BJP-led government of Assam in 2016 declared that the state-run madrasas (religious educational institution of Muslims) would remain open on Fridays that has so far been a weekly holiday in these institutions. It argued that the

[5] This special concession is granted in various parts of the country, Bihar and West Bengal in particular.

[6] In 2014, the BJP-led NDA government at the centre announced to hold 'Good Governance Day' to honour and mark the birth anniversary of the former Prime Minister of India, Atal Bihar Vajpayee, who also happened to be the first prime minister belonging to the BJP.

[7] In another controversy, the objection of Justice Kurian Joseph to the decision of the Chief Justice of India (CJI) to hold a meeting of State Chief Justices on Good Friday raised public attention to this issue of holding a meeting on the day of a national holiday of the Christian community. In his letter addressed to the CJI, Justice Kurian Joseph held in unambiguous terms that since these were national holidays and also days of prayer for the Christian community holding a meeting on these days was inappropriate. See DeSouza (2018a) for an in-depth discussion on this issue.

[8] The year 2014 marks a watershed moment in the postcolonial political history of India. For the first time, the BJP, whose political ideology rests on cultural nationalism, came to power at the Centre with a massive mandate. It also won assembly elections in most of the states where elections were held between 2014 and 2018.

move was to bring in uniformity in the weekly holiday pattern followed by the schools (Kashyap, 2016). But this argument, as was expected, did not cut much ice with the members of the Muslim community. Instead, they took the government's decree of scrapping the long tradition (since the 1930s) of Fridays as weekly off days in madrasas as a deliberate assault on their religious and cultural sensibilities. To many the notification forcing government aided madrasas to remain open on Fridays was not merely an act of arm twisting on the part of the government but was also in clear violation of Articles 29 and 30 of the Constitution that guarantee minorities rights to their culture, considering the fact that no law in the country declares Sunday as a holiday (Misra, 2016).

Such seemingly unsettling activities have also been undertaken in other states. In Uttar Pradesh, for example, while the BJP-led government has not tinkered with the observance of Friday as a weekly off day in the state-aided madrasas, it has reduced the number of holidays being observed around Muslim festivals. Besides, as many as ten discretionary holidays previously given to madrasas have also been scrapped. Unsurprisingly, the move of the Uttar Pradesh government drew ample flak from the members of the Muslim communities.[9]

State Financial Support for Religious and Cultural Activities

Financial support for religious activities from the public fund has long been a much-debated issue surrounding the relationship between the State and religion. In particular, it has been the basis of heated philosophical, political and legal debates in many secular democratic nations. In such debates, secularism is often used either to reject or to support public funding of religious and cultural activities. As a result, there is a range of positions with regard to secularity across contemporary secular nation-states—ranging from regimes with very high commitment to secularism to more accommodationist regimes, to ones that remain

[9] See Husain, Ushra. (2018). 'UP Madrasas Told to Cut Muslim Holidays', *Times of India*. Available at https://timesofindia.indiatimes.com/india/up-madrassas-told-to-cut-muslim-holidays/articleshow/62344376.cms (accessed on 21 June 2019).

committed to neutrality of the State but allow high level of cooperation with religions (Martinez-Torron and Durham, 2010; Messner, 2015).

These varied positions have redefined the notion of 'neutrality'. At least three modes of neutrality can be identified: 'exclusive', 'inclusive' and 'compensational'. Basically, the exclusive form of neutrality implies excluding religious manifestations from the public domain whereas the inclusive mode of neutrality includes religious manifestations (of all faiths) in public domains in order to be neutral. The compensational from of neutrality involves the possibility of positive actions, intending to allow religious practices and activities to be accommodated with a view to let them function or enjoy rights on the same, equal footing as others; or to create opportunities and facilities through which freedom of religion can actually be experienced.

As the Indian constitution does not declare any religion to be the religion of the State, religion has no substantive role to play in the affairs of the State. But at the same time, there is no ban on allowing it a ceremonial role in State functions and official events. Conversely, the State is not at all prevented by law from playing a role in the affairs of religion (Mahmood, 2010). Constitutionally, while there is no preferred religion of the State, yet certain denominational Hindu temples in two states—Kerala and Tamil Nadu—receive prescribed subsidies from the public fund and that too by a constitutional dictate.[10] The following observation by Tahir Mahmood[11] very

[10] See Article 290-A which says:

> A sum of forty-six lakhs and fifty thousand rupees shall be charged on, and paid out of, the Consolidated Fund of the State of Kerala every year to the Travancore Devaswom Fund; and a sum of thirteen lakhs and fifty thousand rupees shall be charged on, and paid out of, the Consolidated Fund of the State of Tamil Nadu every year to the Devaswom Fund established in that State for the maintenance of Hindu temples and shrines in the territories transferred to that State on the 1st day of November, 1956, from the State of Travancore-Cochin.

[11] Tahir Mahmood is a renowned jurist specialising in religion and law, and law relating to minorities. He has also served as Member, Law Commission; Member, National Human Rights Commission; Chairman, National Commission for Minorities.

succinctly sums up the relationship between the State and religion in India:

> There is no provision in the Constitution directing the State to remain neutral to religious issues; nor does it specifically ask the State to cooperate with religious communities in respect to their faith affairs. The mandate is only for non-discrimination between people on religious grounds. The silence of the Constitution on this issue is taken as tacit approval for State intervention in religious affairs of all communities and all organs of the State—legislature, executive and judiciary—have accordingly been taking active interest in such affairs in such a way that may be inconceivable under a rigidly secular political set up. (Mahmood, 2010, p. 389)

In brief, secularism in India has broadly come to mean religious equidistance, and not non-involvement of the State (Bhargava, 2010; Varshney, 2002). On various occasions, the court has also clarified that Indian secularism requires that the State's role with respect to different religions should be one of benevolent neutrality.[12] Seen thus, the notion of State neutrality with respect to religion in India fits both inclusive and compensational forms of neutrality (as discussed previously).

In practice, the Indian State over the past 70 years has deployed its resources, financial or otherwise, for religious activities and in a variety of ways. These include but are not limited to the following.[13] First, the State spends on preservation and maintenance of monuments including religious structures. For example, as far back as 1951, the Gujarat government provided money to rebuild the Somnath temple (Khalidi, 2008). Similarly, the State has spent money from its exchequer on the preservation and maintenance of many old religious structures of Islamic and other faiths (Mahmood, 2010).

---

[12] S.R. Bommai vs. Union of India, [1994] 3 S. C. C. 1.

[13] Khalidi (2008) presents a long list of religious activities that are funded from the State exchequer.

Second, many state governments have long been funding, partially or fully, religious institutions such as madrasas. The Central Government too provides financial support to these religious institutions for various purposes. The most notable example of this is Central Government's modernisation of madrasa scheme. Third, religious endowments of all communities enjoy certain exemptions under tax laws. Moreover, in many cases, there are State appointed and financially supported bodies to oversee their management. Fourth, the State has also subsidised celebration of religious festivals and figures. For example, public money has been spent on organising *Kumbh Mela*[14] and on making special arrangements/ facilities for celebrating certain religious festivals.[15] In the past, the State had also subsidised celebration of centenaries of the founders of Sikh and Jain religions. Fifth, there is also no ban on the State providing financial and logistic support for pilgrimage within and outside India. For instance, the Central, as well as many state governments, have long been subsidising *Haj* pilgrimage to Mecca, the epicentre of the Muslim universe, until it was scrapped in 2018 (see Box 4.1). In many states, there are schemes for subsidising pilgrimage for pilgrims of other faiths namely Hinduism under which the governments provide money to resident devotees going on the Mansarovar Yatra, Amarnath Yatra and so on.[16] Similarly, for Sikhs, special arrangements have been made for pilgrimages to Nankana Sahib and Panja Sahib in Pakistan (Aiyer, 2006).

[14] The Kumbh Mela is a mass pilgrimage in which the followers of Hinduism gather to bathe in the holy river. In the last Kumbh Mela held in 2013, an amount of ₹ 1,300 crore was spent. The UPA government at the Centre had pitched in with ₹ 1,013 crore. The remaining amount was borne by the State government of Uttar Pradesh.

[15] For example, the Uttar Pradesh Government in its budget for the financial year 2018–2019 separately earmarked a fund of ₹ 10 crore for celebrating Diwali and Holi festivals.

[16] For example, in many states like Chhattisgarh, Delhi, Madhya Pradesh, Uttar Pradesh and Uttarakhand there is a scheme called *Mukhya Mantri Tirtha Yatra Yojna* (Chief Minister's pilgrimage scheme) under which financial support is given to Hindu pilgrims.

While public funding of religious and cultural activities has been a practice for long, it has not been without contestation at multiple levels—though much of it has been around activities associated with the minorities. The subsidies given to Muslims for Haj pilgrimage have been at the heart of the polemics of public funding of religious activities. At the institutional level, it has been challenged in the court of law. A petition seeking to challenge the Haj Committees Act (2002) the provisions of which allegedly allowed the Central and State Governments to give grants to the Haj Committees to subsidise air travel for Haj pilgrims was filed in the Supreme Court in 2007. In 2011, the court dismissed the petition (Prafull Goradia vs. The Union of India)[17] on two grounds: First, there was no discrimination on the basis of religion as the state subsidised pilgrims of other religions. Second, as only a small portion of the taxes levied were used for this purpose, it would not violate Article 27 of the Constitution.[18] To put it a bit differently, public funding of religious activities would amount to such a violation only if a 'substantial part of taxpayer money' were to be used to promote religious activity.[19] In 2012, a two-judge bench of the Supreme Court, however, directed the Central Government to gradually reduce and abolish Haj subsidy in 10 years. Curiously enough, the court agreed that the subsidy was 'constitutionally valid' and yet it pronounced that 'Haj subsidy is something that is best done away with'. In this matter, the court, thus, did not base its verdict on

[17] Prafull Goradia vs. The Union of India (2011), 2 SCC 568.

[18] Article 27 of the Constitution states that: 'No person shall be compelled to pay any taxes, the proceeds of which are specifically appropriated in payment of expenses for the promotion or maintenance of any particular religion or religious denomination.'

[19] The Supreme Court held:

> In our opinion Article 27 would be violated if a substantial part of the entire income tax collected in India, or a substantial part of the entire central excise or the customs duties or sales tax, or a substantial part of any other tax collected in India, were to be utilized for promotion or maintenance of any particular religion or religious denomination. In other words, suppose 25 percent of the entire income tax collected in India was utilized for promoting or maintaining any particular religion or religious denomination, that, in our opinion, would be violative of Article 27 of the Constitution.

legal principles, rather anchored it in the text of Holy Quran that suggests: 'Haj (pilgrimage to Makkah) to the House (Ka'bah) is a duty that mankind owes to Allah, those who can afford the expenses (for one's conveyance, provision and residence)'.[20]

The issue of public funding for religious activities has been contested in the political arena as well. As a matter of fact, it has triggered acrimonious political debates. But such debates are often ambivalent as they eventually boil down to targeting activities associated with the minority communities. Consider, for example, the Haj subsidy, which has long been under attack, especially from the Hindu Rights. It has been projected as part of the package of 'minority appeasement' policy put in place by the so-called secular, or rather pro-minority political parties in order to secure electoral support of minorities. This particular issue along with others such as a Uniform Civil Code (UCC) has constantly been used by the BJP and its sister organisations for electoral mobilisation of the majority community, which in turn, it is claimed, has provided the party considerable support among the Hindu voters (Misra, 2011).

Box 4.1: The Saga of Haj Subsidy: At a Glance

The Haj pilgrimage is organised annually during which Muslim pilgrims visit Mecca and other places in Saudi Arabia, often regarded as the epicentre of Muslim universe. Saudi Arabia allocates a quota to each country on the basis of one pilgrim per thousand of the Muslim population of the country. Between 2012 and 2017, a total of 6,71,388 Muslims had gone on Haj pilgrimage through the Haj Committee of India (HCOI) and 2,12,490 through Private Tour Operators (PTOs). The total number of pilgrims was close to 1.7 lakh in 2012 and had dropped to around 1.36 lakh in 2013. The quota remained at 1.36 lakh till 2016. In the year 2017, the quota increased to 1.7 lakh pilgrims.

The Haj subsidy was introduced in the colonial times, around early 1930s, when the British colonial regime provided for a government-funded Haj committee and named Bombay and Calcutta as two ports

[20] Many legal experts expressed their dissatisfaction and questioned the verdict. Also see, Dhamija (2012).

from where Muslims could embark upon their pilgrimage. Post-independence, the government replaced the previous Act in 1959. In the new Act, a committee was constituted in Bombay to take care of all affairs of the pilgrims, including travel arrangements during the pilgrimage and to cover overhead expenses. The Committee Act was further modified in 1973 when the mode of travel to Saudi Arabia was changed from sea to air, owing to rising oil prices. Accordingly, the government also increased the subsidy to cover the difference between sea and airfares. Till 1995, about 5,000 pilgrims used to travel by sea, while around 19,000 used to travel by air each year. However, in 1995 sea travel was completely discarded and all pilgrims had to use air transport. According to some sources, the total subsidy amount by the government was to the tune of ₹ 837 crores in 2012, which decreased to ₹ 405 crores in 2016.

It is, however, important to note that Air India is the only option for the Haj pilgrims, to take a flight to Saudi Arabia, for performing the annual pilgrimage, through various Haj Committees. It, thus, means that such a monetary help, doled out by the government, goes to the coffers of the official air carrier and not to the pockets of the pilgrims, as the popular impression may be. Given this, it is claimed that Air India charges a higher price from Haj pilgrims, in comparison to normal passengers. In other words, the so-called Haj subsidy is a pretention, in disguise, to support Air India, to compensate for its loss. Many critics of the subsidy hold that, if booked months in advance, it is possible to buy cheaper air tickets, thereby doing away with the need for subsidy.

The Haj subsidy has been in the eye of the political storm. The Hindutva forces have always opposed it; castigated it as 'minority appeasement' and as 'symbol of pseudo-secularism', and made an issue in elections. Many Muslims have also risen against it as Haj is a kind of worship, compulsory for only those Muslims, who can afford it (both wealth wise and health-wise, and that too once in a lifetime).

In 2012, a two-judge bench of Supreme Court directed the Haj subsidy to be gradually phased out in the coming ten years. In 2017, a Central Haj Committee meeting decided to do away with the subsidy by the following year. Following up on this, the Government of India announced to scrap Haj subsidy in 2018.

Sources: Mishra (2011) and Shamshi (2018).

Iconography

All societies across the globe have tended to utilise their pasts as social, cultural and political resources. An important means by which societies have done this is through the naming/renaming of towns, cities, streets and roads in particular (Whelan, 2005). However, the toponomic significance of naming places, especially to honour public figures, has been interpreted variously: (a) as indicators of nationalistic fervours (Stump, 1988; Zelinsky, 1983); (b) as ideological tools to divest landscapes of its colonial association and acquire political legitimation (Lewandowski, 1984); (c) as markers of social and power relations of deference and defiance upon which naming is contingent (Pirie, 1984) and (d) as signifiers of heritage. Briefly put, the naming of place, whether as a conscious event or a more informal process of evolution, is, in different ways and varying degrees, associated with sociopolitical activity which embodies some of the social struggle for control over the means of symbolic production and representation within the built environment (Pirie, 1984; Yeoh, 1996).

In pluralistic societies, symbols are what unite and divide people. Therefore, the symbols that a multi-ethnic and/or multicultural nation chooses to retain, aid and erase are not only reflective of what kind of history it makes or remakes but also of the direction in which it moves (from monocultural to multicultural or vice versa). In this context, it would be interesting to map the namescapes in India, a complex multi-ethnic, multi-religious and multicultural society so as to be able to fathom if and how far the iconography of the nation reflects the multi-religious and multicultural context of the society. However, the discussion that follows is confined to naming and renaming of streets/roads only and is primarily focused on Delhi—the political and cultural seat of many empires over the centuries.

Affixing names to streets/roads take on great symbolic as well as functional significance (Whelan, 2005). While little is known about the naming processes and procedures, street or place names during the Moghul period drew largely on natural characteristics such as geography, shape and size; although streets and places were also named after Kings/Queens and in some cases based on functional use in terms of economic activity. But the British colonial period marked an important shift. Not only did the British formalise the processes of naming of streets/roads, places and public buildings, it named vast chunks of streets after resident Viceroys, councillors and important functionaries of the colonial power (for example, Irwin Road, Curzon Road, Hardinge Avenue, etc.). Interestingly, the procedures of naming places/streets/roads, etc. would not lose sight of the nuances. While selecting streets/roads for honouring a person utmost care would be taken to reflect that the chosen street/road was commensurate with the esteem due to the person (Nidhi, 2017).

A prolonged battle against the British regime produced new icons and heroes who were to be honoured after the colonial power was dismantled and a new political era had dawned. As expected, India after independence embarked on naming the streets/roads mostly after freedom fighters, eminent personalities and local icons across the social spectrum. Nevertheless, a flurry of demands for relabelling existing names of streets/roads created problems as much of it actually sought to meddle with history. The city of Delhi offers an important case study in this context.

The city of Delhi has been the political and cultural seat of many empires. In turn, each of these empires shaped and left their imprints on the built-in environment as well as cultural landscapes of the city (Jain, 1990; Singh and Varma, 2001). At the time of independence, the names of streets and roads that crisscrossed the city presented a living text of the multilayered past. Named after Ashoka or Akbar or Chelmsford, the streets/roads of Lutyens' Delhi (New Delhi)[21] reflected the span of history from ancient to

[21] New Delhi was designed by British architect Sir Edwin Landseer Lutyens along with Sir Herbert Baker from 1911 to 1931.

Moghul to British era. Immediately after independence, many streets/roads were named to honour the freedom fighters, political leaders and eminent personalities from different walks of life and across socioreligious communities. However, the nationalistic fervours also sought to change the existing names. In the changed political climate, the first victims were the names associated with the colonial past. Unsurprisingly then, the names of many streets/roads that were named after the British Viceroys and officials were replaced by the new ones (see Box 4.2). But the zeal of changing names of certain streets/roads was so overwhelming that it led the Government of India to issue guidelines for naming/renaming the streets/roads. As per the guidelines: (a) name of existing streets/roads, etc. should not be changed; only new ones and such old streets/roads, etc. as are in existence without specific names may be named after eminent personalities—local, national or international—to honour them; (b) once the street/road has been named after a particular dignitary then a fresh proposal for renaming should not be sent to the Street Names Authority; (c) names which are part of history may not be altered; (d) any renaming can be considered by the Council only when there are directions from the Government of India; (e) renaming can only be an exception and recommendations in this regard can be given by the Council and any contrary decision of the Government of India shall be brought to the notice of the Council.[22] Of all, two points of the guidelines are the most salient ones. First, changing existing names as per the guidelines is something that can rarely be done. Second, no alteration can be done to names that are part of or are associated with history. However, the guidelines have been violated and attempts made to meddle with history more than once (see Box 4.2).

[22] Ministry of Home Affairs, Government of India, vide letter No. 13022/34/74- Delhi dated 27.9.1975.

Box 4.2: Renaming Streets/Roads in Delhi: Post 1947

Old Names	*New Names*
Allenby Road	Dr. Bishambhar Das Marg
Baird Road	Bangla Sahib Marg
Clive road	Thyagaraja Marg
Cornwallis Road	Subramania Bharti Marg
Curzon Road	Kasturba Gandhi Marg
Elgin Road	Netaji Subhash Marg
Havelock Road	Kalibari Marg
Hardinge Avenue	Tilak Marg
Irwin Road	Baba Kharak Singh Marg
Kingsway	Rajpath
King Edward Road	Maulana Azad Road
Kitchener Road	Sardar Patel Marg
Queensway	Janpath
Race Course Road	Lok Kalyan Road
Reading Road	Mandir Marg
Robert's Robert Road	Teen Murti Road
Wellesley Road	Zakir Hussain Marg

Source: Compiled by the authors.

While renaming streets/roads in 1950s was used as an ideological tool to divest landscapes of their colonial association and acquire political legitimation, a new trend seems to have set in with the rise of cultural nationalists in political power in recent years. Renaming of streets, roads and places is now being used to polarise socioreligious communities for electoral advantage. The most visible pattern is picking up streets/roads/places bearing association with medieval period—often seen by the cultural nationalists as a period of political and cultural rupture—and renaming them.

The most controversial case in this context is renaming Aurangzeb Road in 2015 after A.P.J. Abdul Kalam—one of the most popular former Presidents of India. This particular instance of renaming or relabelling of one of the most important roads of Central Delhi is of enormous symbolic and political significance. For one thing, Aurangzeb, one of the most powerful Moghul rulers, is seen by many, mostly the Hindu right as the symbol of 'Islamic fanaticism' and 'despotism'. On the other hand, A.P.J. Abdul Kalam, though a devout Muslim himself, is hailed as a kind and benevolent human being and above all an illustrious son of the soil who, through his momentous contribution in India's defence sector was described as the 'missile man' and added to the strength and pride of the country. In a way, relabelling Aurangzeb Road after A.P.J. Abdul Kalam is not only an attempt of further excoriating Aurangzeb but also of playing the politics of 'Good Muslim/Bad Muslim'.

This is, however, not an isolated case but rather confirms a pattern. For instance, a 150-year-old railway station named 'Mughal Sarai' (in the state of Uttar Pradesh) has recently been renamed as 'Pt. Deen Dayal Upadhyaya Junction' after the Jan Sangh (the precursor to the BJP) leader Deen Dayal Upadhyaya. The city of Allahabad named by Akbar (who, unlike Aurangzeb, is hailed as a benevolent and secular Moghul king) has been renamed as Prayagraj. Even the famous Hazratganj Crossing in Lucknow, named after Begum Hazrat Mahal, a heroic Avadh queen who fought the British, has been declared to be renamed as 'Atal Chowk'—after one of the founding members of the BJP and the former Prime Minister of India. What is, however, more worrisome is that all this did not arouse strong enough public outcry so as to stop government's renaming spree. There is a little realisation that renaming places, streets or roads creates ruptures in people's lived experience. It is also like demolishing monuments. Once erased, they fade from public memory and consciousness.

Educational Policies

In modern times, the education system of a country is not merely a site of production and transmission of knowledge and of socio-economically useful skills but also one of the primary agencies of socialisation. It is in educational institutions, schools in particular, that the children learn about and develop attitudes towards the nation, the society and the outside world. Generally speaking, education systems seek to transmit the dominant value system to the next generation. This is hardly an issue in homogeneous societies (Watson, 1979). But in ethnically/culturally pluralistic societies the educational systems must have different orientations. In many contexts not only does it have to respond to the issues of equity and social justice for the members of disadvantaged minorities, it may also have to be pro-active to how core values of minority groups are presented and represented in educational processes.[23] In brief, educational policies across the world are quite variable in their approaches to the educational needs and aspirations of minorities and to the introduction of their culture and language in educational spaces, contents and processes (see Box 4.3). In the following analysis, we look at whether and how far the Indian educational policy has taken care of all of these.

Curriculum and Textbooks

The centrality of curriculum and school textbooks in social sciences to build a national imaginary cannot be overemphasised. We can see that across a range of countries. For instance, the excesses of colonialism and slavery, it is held, do not find adequate treatment in school textbooks of the erstwhile colonial powers. Similarly, the fact that the abolition of slavery resulted in a policy where the state compensated the slave owners for their loss of property and such compensation continued well into the twentieth century is not a well-known fact (Olusoga, 2018; Willsher, 2010). Given this, what enters the curriculum framework, as well as textbooks, is determined by the dominant narrative fostered by the ruling elite in tandem with the social groups in control of both symbolic and

---

[23] What constitutes core value of a group depends on what shapes and undergirds its collective identity. For instance, for a group, its core value may be represented by its native language; for another it may be represented by religion; or race; or colour; or even by clan or sect. In some cases, core value of a group may combine more than one of these attributes.

Box 4.3: Minorities and Educational Policy Approaches

Policy Approaches	*Aim*	*Exemplar*[24]
Recognition approach	The state formally recognises the rights of minority languages, culture and education, and educational policy seeks to reflect the same.	India, Former USSR
Unification approach	The educational policy seeks to create a unified sense of nationhood using a national language of instruction, and centrally prescribed textbooks and curricula.	Chad, Ghana, Indonesia, Malaysia, Sudan, Tanzania
Separation approach	While the educational policy aims at developing a common nationality, at the same time it allows for preserving different languages and culture of minority groups. It also provides schooling through different language media.	Singapore, Nigeria
Integration approach	The state through the school system seeks to integrate the minorities into the mainstream of homogeneous society.	Australia, USA, France
Laissez-Faire approach	No official policy; decision being left to individual local authorities.	United Kingdom, Germany

Source: Based on the typology provided by Watson (1979).

material wealth of the society and political power (Apple, 1990). As a result, quite often the content and process of schooling in plural societies constitute an important site of conflict between the dominant and the dominated (for example, minority) groups over the production of knowledge, ideology and culture. As we shall see in the following discussion, India is no exception to this.

[24] It is, however, important to note that there has been a marked shift in policy approach in many of these countries. For instance, in many countries like USA and Australia, there is now more emphasis on a policy of cultural pluralism than on a policy of integration/assimilation. Similarly, the United Kingdom has moved from laissez-faire approach to formal and structured one.

In the Constitutional scheme of India, education initially constituted one of the items of State subjects,[25] which meant that the state governments would be solely responsible for taking all decisions pertaining to education, including the curricula. As a result, the contents and forms of schooling and standards of education varied across, and in some cases, even within the states. There was, therefore, as such no formal national curriculum framework in place until 1976. This was also roughly the period of time in the postcolonial political history of India that marked the dominance of the Congress Party on the political scene. Since most of the state governments in those days were headed by the Congress Party that had adopted a secular cultural policy, the knowledge and appreciation of cultural diversity would generally inform and undergird the curriculum design. It was probably for this reason that no need was felt for framing and putting in place a formal National Curriculum Framework (NCF) that would guide the curriculum design at the sub-national level.

However, the political dominance of the Congress Party began to decline in the 1970s. As it lost power in a number of states around this time, the Congress still a ruling party at the centre undertook a series of measures. In the field of education, the National Council of Educational Research and Training (NCERT)[26] was assigned the task of framing the first National Curriculum Framework (NCF), which appeared in 1975. It was followed by an amendment to the Constitution (the 42nd Constitutional Amendment Act, 1976)

[25] The Constitution of India provides for the division of power between the Union (Central) and State governments. All the subjects are arranged in three lists—Union, State and Concurrent. The Union List includes those subjects over which the central government has exclusive power to legislate. The State List describes those subjects over which the state governments have the powers to legislate and enact policies. Finally, the Concurrent List includes those subjects which are the joint jurisdiction of both the central and the state governments.

[26] National Council of Educational Research and Training (NCERT) was established in 1960s as an apex national level body to frame curriculum framework and prepare model textbooks at school level and also to facilitate teacher training and research.

to bring education under the Concurrent List so that the central government (along with the state governments) would be able to intervene in and legislate on educational matters. All this occurred not for nothing but for the accumulated evidence that the school curricula plays a momentous role in shaping the minds of students with implications for the process of nation-building.

As education in the early decades of independence was seen to play a central role in nation building and modernising the nation, the school curriculum constituted an important instrument of social change; of inculcating Constitutional values of plurality, an open society that was democratic, secular and socialist (Batra, 2015). It is, therefore, not surprising that the first NCF (NCERT, 1975) reflected all of this in its structure and content. For instance, the NCF (NCERT, 1975) in its general objectives stressed on 'awakening of social consciousness, democratic values and a feeling for social justice and national integration'. It further mentioned that 'national integration can be achieved only through a proper understanding and appreciation of different *sub-cultures* of India and common bonds that hold them together', and that 'discrimination of any kind based on sex, caste, religion, language or region is to be looked at with aversion' (emphasis added; NCERT, 1975). Furthermore, even as the first NCF (NCERT, 1975) sought to address diversity along language, culture and tradition, the specific guidelines for history textbooks cautioned against the introduction of local history at the school stage as it often runs the risk of promoting parochialism and regional cultural chauvinism (Batra, 2015).

The National Policy on Education (NPE) that came into being in 1986 not only reiterated and rearticulated the constitutional commitment to educational rights of religious minorities, it also went even a step further to recognise their educational needs and aspirations. It held that:

> Some minority groups are educationally deprived or backward. Greater attention will be paid to the education of these groups in the interest of

> equality and social justice. This will naturally include the Constitutional guarantees given to them to establish and administer their own educational institutions, and protection to their languages and culture. Simultaneously, objectivity will be reflected in the preparation of textbooks and in all school activities, and all possible measures will be taken to promote an integration based on appreciation of common national goals and ideals, in conformity with the core curriculum. (MHRD, 1986, Para 4.8)

However, as soon as the BJP-led National Democratic Alliance (NDA) government came to power in 1999, it decided to draw up and put in place a new NCF. Given the BJP's sociopolitical ideology of 'one nation, one culture', its decision of bringing in a new curriculum sparked controversy and triggered debates. However, much against the anxieties and fear of many, the National Curriculum Framework for School Education (NCFSE) put in place in 2000 also underlined the ideas of cultural pluralism and 'unity in diversity'. The document mentioned:

> Characterised as one of the longest surviving continuum of cultures, India is a multi-cultural and multilingual society with a perennial undercurrent of essential unity.... Like the myriad species of plants and animals that make up the rich natural world, the large number of beliefs, religions and races inhabit one of the geographically most diverse countries. India's various ethnic groups form interconnecting loops, competing and cooperating while forming complex webs of interaction. Indian culture, thus, is a living process assimilating various strands of thought and lifestyle. The process has created a rich collage of India exemplifying 'unity in diversity and diversity in unity'. (NCERT, 2000, pp. 2–3)

But what appeared on the surface to be a curriculum having regard for cultural diversity, on deeper inspection turned out to be privileging the traditions and cultural values of the majority group. Under the garb of value education, its contents actually sought to reinforce traditional knowledge, values, authorities and hierarchies. Through its emphasis on developing a national identity underpinned by the ideas of cultural nationalism, a departure from the Nehruvian commitment of modernity and secularism, the NCFSE (NCERT,

2000) actually sought to present a different idea of India (Kumar, 2000).

As it came under attacks from several quarters, the return of the Congress [under the banner of United Progressive Alliance (UPA)] to power in 2004 paved the way for framing of a new NCF in 2005. With cross-cultural perspective in design, the NCERT (2005, p. 7) held that:

> India is a multicultural society made up of numerous regional and local cultures. People's religious beliefs, ways of life and their understanding of social relationships are quite distinct from another. All the groups have equal rights to co-exist and flourish, and the education system needs to respond to the cultural pluralism inherent in our society. The cultural diversity of this land should continue to be treasured as our special attribute.

With the return of BJP to power in 2014, the battle over the idea of India turned full circle. As soon as the new regime assumed power, various right-wing formations became active and vocal, pressing hard for overhauling the school curriculum.[27] They began to rearticulate traditional, political and cultural themes. They reasserted their old claim that the existing curriculum framed by the left-liberals does not inculcate proper Indian nationalistic values. Nor does it correctly reflect what India has culturally been. While the current political regime has so far been unable to come up with either the new national education policy or a fresh NCF, a fierce campaign for the same is going on.

Even more intense ideological battle (modernism/secularism vs. traditionalism/cultural nationalism) has been fought over

[27] In December 2014, shortly after the formation of the BJP government at the Centre, a national-level conference attended by close to 200 academics and experts was held by the RSS-backed *Shiksha Bachao Andolan* (Save Education Campaign) at Ujjain in Madhya Pradesh. Based on the deliberations, a report was submitted to the Ministry of Human Resource Development (MHRD). As reported in the media, the MHRD has not only welcomed the inputs received from the RSS but has also been meeting almost on regular basis with its affiliates for the so-called 'course correction' in education. See also, Trivedi (2014).

the contents of social science textbooks, of history textbooks in particular. The first generation of history textbooks was written under the aegis of NCERT in 1960s. But controversies began to surround these textbooks as soon as the Congress lost power in 1977. As the Janata Party that replaced the Congress Party at the centre was a conglomeration of smaller political formations with varying ideological persuasions, including those championing cultural nationalism, some constituents of it questioned the contents of the existing textbooks prepared by NCERT. Barely a few months after assuming power, Morarji Desai, the then Prime Minister, received an anonymous memorandum.[28] It alleged, among other things, that the communists had infiltrated important academic institutions and research organisations, including the NCERT. The textbooks prescribed by NCERT were infused with the communist ideology, fostering an image of India far removed from its traditional cultural values. On 28 May 1977, the Principal Secretary to the Prime Minister forwarded a note to the then education minister, P.C. Chunder that mentioned that some textbooks contained controversial and biased material which was prejudicial to the conception of the Indian past; and that the Prime Minister also thought that the education ministry might consider withdrawing these books from circulation. The focus of the controversy was that some of these textbooks explained conflicts among elites primarily in political rather than religious terms, they argued that sufficient space was not given to the resistance put up by Sikhs and Rajputs against Muslims and the textbooks only focused on the brighter side of the Moghul rule in India (Nair, 2010; Rudolph and Rudolph, 1983). In brief, the history textbooks in question did not suit a right-wing interpretation of Indian history. Since the Janata Party-led government was short-

[28] Given the nature of allegation, it could be surmised that the memorandum was sent by those associated with right-wing formations. In some circles, it was suspected that the memorandum was sent by Nanaji Deshmukh, the leader of the Jan Sangh, a right-wing formation (Nair, 2010).

lived, the books at the centre of controversy could not be completely withdrawn though their circulation was restricted.

History textbooks again became the subject of controversy as soon as the BJP-led NDA government assumed power in 1999. New textbooks were published and introduced in 2003. The history books, among other things, uncritically glorified the ancient period of Indian history (Roy, 2002), de-emphasised and denigrated the medieval period (Nair, 2010) that was an era of political rule by invaders and cultural outsiders in the imaginations of Hindu nationalists and also showed some religious minorities (Muslims and Sikhs in particular) in poor light in the context of communal violence and terrorism (Banerjee and Stober, 2014). This outraged a section of educationists, intellectuals and civil society activists who termed it a blatant exercise of rewriting of history textbooks as 'saffronisation' and 'communalisation'. As was to be expected, no sooner did the UPA government come to power in 2004 that the process of 'de-saffronisation' or 'detoxification' of history texts was set in motion under the rubric of 'course correction'. This effectively meant withdrawal of the allegedly distorted and communalised textbooks, leading to the production of a third generation of textbooks (that appeared between 2006 and 2008) retaining the spirit and flavour of the first-generation textbooks.

The wheel has turned again with BJP's coming back to power in 2014. Given its past record of tinkering with textbooks to suit its sociopolitical ideology, the left-liberal intellectuals, as well as secularists, feared that the social science textbooks, especially the history textbooks, would be rewritten or replaced. As a matter of fact, revision of textbooks has already been carried out especially in social science textbooks—history, political science and economics. For instance, in history textbooks for classes sixth to tenth, as reported in the media, there is more emphasis on the ancient Indian philosophy and the knowledge system. Furthermore, larger space has been given to the icons who, according to the cultural nationalists, contributed to or fought for India's, more accurately, for Hindus' pride (Chopra,

2018). In the revised textbooks of political science for Class 12 students, the word 'anti-Muslim' is reported to have been dropped when describing the 2002 riots that took place in Gujarat. In the chapter titled 'Politics in India since Independence' the passage in the old book read, 'In February-March 2002, large-scale violence against Muslims took place in Gujarat'. However, in the revised edition, the same passage reads as, 'In February-March 2002, large-scale violence took place in Gujarat'. All of this is said to have been done without following due procedures, such as the consultation with the Textbook Development Committees and authors of respective textbooks which has hitherto been an established practice for carrying out the revision of textbooks (Vasudevan, 2018).

Even more blatant revision of textbooks is made in the states ruled by the BJP. In Maharashtra, for instance, the history textbook meant for Grade X earlier comprised chapters on Moghul emperors and their contribution, besides a detailed history of events that impacted Western countries, such as the French Revolution, Greek philosophy, the American War of Independence, etc. All of this has now either been discarded or reduced to a few lines. In Rajasthan, another BJP-ruled State, textbooks on social sciences have been revised to an extent where cultural nationalists such as V.D. Savarkar have been given significant space, sidelining prominent liberal and secular faces including M.K. Gandhi and Jawaharlal Nehru but also to the extent of showing the medieval period (in which Muslims ruled the greater part of India) in a poor light.

Clearly, the battle over curriculum and textbooks reflects the tensions that underlie competing imaginations of the Indian nation. Broadly speaking, on the one side of the divide are those who emphasise modernism, pluralism and inclusiveness. On the other side are the advocates of traditionalism, cultural nationalism and exclusivism, seeking to project minorities as 'troublesome' (as referred to in the chapter 'Introduction: Pluralism and Democracy'), to degrade their icons and cultural values and to downplay the contribution of the minorities to nation building as well as national life.

Medium of Instruction

In a plural society, as mentioned at the outset of this section, language may also constitute part of the core values of different groups. And hence, it often becomes a site of the power play as some linguistic varieties and practices are considered to be superior and legitimate whereas others are considered as inferior and thus are to be ignored if not erased completely (Bourdieu, 1991; Heller and Martin-Jones, 2001). In most multilingual societies, the trend is one of homogenising in complex ways. As Blackledge (2008) points out:

> Very often, multilingual societies that apparently tolerate or promote heterogeneity in fact undervalue or appear to ignore the linguistic diversity of their populace. An apparently liberal orientation to equality of opportunity for all may mask an ideological drive towards homogeneity, a drive which potentially marginalizes or excludes those who either refuse, or are unwilling, to conform.

India, being home of thousands of dialects and languages,[29] has long grappled with the issue of language in various arenas.[30] The intense, often polarised, debates around official language and mother tongue have played a crucial role in shaping educational policies (Groff, 2013; Rao, 2008; Sridhar, 1996). The question of what language ought to be

[29] Estimates on the number of languages being spoken in India abound. For instance, the Census of India (2001) reported 122 languages across 28 states. Of these languages, 22 are listed in the Constitution and called as Scheduled languages. It also listed 1,635 mother tongues, as well as 1,957 unclassified 'other' mother tongues. As per the *Ethnologue*, as many as 447 languages are still spoken in India (Lewis, Gary and Charles, 2014). However, the most recent People's Linguistic Survey of India (Bhasha Research and Publication Centre, 2017) listed 780 living languages in India.

[30] Although the language question became a matter of intense debates during the colonial period in the contexts of the relationship between and among speech communities and medium of education, it assumed greater importance just after independence in 1947. In the 1950s, the political map of India was virtually redrawn on the basis of language. The issue of official language in the 1960s turned violent and as a result, three language formula was devised to resolve it. In education, the three-language formula (with modification in 1966) has been worked out as follows: first, the mother tongue or regional language to be taught for ten years; second, the official language—Hindi or English—to be taught for six years minimum; third, another modern Indian or foreign language to be taught for three years minimum. Also see Brass (1994, [1974]2005); Groff (2013); Sarangi (2010).

the medium of instruction at various levels of education, as we shall see in the following discussion, continues to remain an issue and a matter of debate.

The Constitution of India declares that the federal states would endeavour to provide adequate facilities for instruction in the mother tongue at the stage of primary education. Article 350-A of the Constitution states that:

> It should be the endeavour of every State and of every local authority within the State to provide adequate facilities for instruction in the mother tongue at the primary stage of education to children belonging to linguistic minority groups; and the President may issue such directions to any State as he considers necessary or proper for securing the provision for such facilities.

More recently, the NCF (NCERT, 2005) and the *Right to Education Act* (2009) have reaffirmed the importance of mother tongue as medium of instruction in schools. Although the notion of mother tongue has all along been surrounded by controversies and hence has been problematic for various reasons,[31] the translation of the term 'adequate facilities' meant that arrangements must be made for instruction in the mother tongue by appointing one teacher provided there are not fewer than 40 pupils speaking the language in the whole school or 10 such pupils in a class.

As the official policy of the government of India as well as the state governments have adhered to the principle of using the mother tongue as the medium of instruction at least in the initial stages, three types of schools are provided. The first type is the one where the 'principal' medium is the official language of the state (the majority of schools

[31] For example, Dua (1986: 135) suggests that sometimes 'the notion of mother tongue has been mixed up with region, religion, profession, ethnicity, caste names and the like'. Second, the official definition of mother tongue has changed over the years, ranging from the 'language spoken by the parents', 'language of general use', and 'language spoken by the mother' (also see Pattanayak, 2003). Third, the official language of the state is, more often than not, conflated with mother tongue.

are of this type). The second type includes those schools where a minority language is used as the medium of instruction whenever there are at least 10 students in a given class who request it. The third type of schools are the ones where a minority language is used as the primary medium in the entire school (usually these schools are either run by minority institutions, or by state governments in areas with a substantial presence of minorities).

On the face of it, the language policy of India is exceptionally multilingual and in sharp contrast with many democratic multilingual/ multicultural nations which have either consciously sought to be monolingual or desisted from recognising and promoting minority languages. In reality, however, dominant languages have become even more dominant or hegemonic in India. There is enough evidence to suggest that over the years the spectrum of languages in schools has been shrinking. For instance, at the primary stage, the number of languages used in schools has come down from 43 in 1986 to 33 in 1993. In all other stages of education too, the number of languages as the media of instruction has reduced significantly (NCERT, 1986, 1993). Clearly, this state of affairs points to the glaring failure of India's language policy.

The reason for the constantly declining number of languages used in schools as mother tongues is often attributed, in part, to operational difficulties (the main hindrances being lack of availability of multilingual teachers and texts) and, in part, to rising aspiration of minority parents to educate their wards in high status languages for social and economic advancement. All this has, however, been contested as apologies for not being able to implement the policy on mother tongue as a medium of instruction in both letter and spirit. For instance, Dua (1985, p. 172) argues that much of the successful implementation, or lack of it, of mother tongue policy depends on various sociopolitical and sociolinguistic factors. The use of minority languages in education faces implementation problems due not so much to lack of student motivation and ability or from the parents' devaluation of such instruction, but owing to pedagogic, environmental and curricular problems. Added to this is the 'mistrust' of implementing agencies that render implementation of the policy ineffective as some administrators fear that meeting the demand of mother tongue will lead to more demands from the minority groups and community members (Annamalai, 1990).

With the notable exception of Sikhs, India's religious minorities do not constitute as both faith and linguistic communities as they do not speak languages distinct from that of the majority community in the given spatial contexts. As for Sikhs, they are largely concentrated in the state of Punjab and do form the majority community there, and hence Gurumukhi, the language spoken by them, does not face deliberate neglect or discrimination.

Although many Muslims claim 'Urdu' as their mother tongue in northern India, Urdu in its standard form is hardly spoken by common masses of the community. Yet, many Muslims in this part of the country wish to have their children schooled in the Urdu medium. But Urdu is said to have received a raw deal by the state governments at multiple levels (Farouqui, 1994).[32] One, slowly but gradually Urdu has been driven out of school as a medium of instruction. Two, even where Muslims constitute the bulk of student community there is a pathetic lack of Urdu teachers. Third, pedagogic materials including textbooks in Urdu often face chronic short supply. The lack of facilities in teaching in Urdu is not only held as a major obstacle to academic progress and achievement of students belonging to the community (Hamid, 1987) but also seen as a surreptitious way of pushing many children to religious seminaries, the only educational site available to the community that preserves its cultural values, traditions and practices (Alam, 2012).

---

[32] For an insightful discussion on politics around Urdu in postcolonial India, see Farouqui (2006).

Box 4.4: Language in Education Planning in Postcolonial India: A Chronology

1947: An Expert Committee of the Indian National Congress made a recommendation for the protection of minorities who would not be kept from developing their languages, but also for government support in providing facilities for mother-tongue education if a non-regional language is used by a significant proportion of the population.

1948: The National Planning Committee on General Education and Technical Education and Developmental Research reported that the time and energy of the students were diverted by the use of English and that the mother-tongue should be used at the secondary level.

1949: The Central Advisory Board of Education (CABE) and the State Education Ministers' Conference stated that at the primary stage mother-tongue instruction should be provided for linguistic minorities with 40 or more students in a school or 10 in a class.

1952: The Secondary Education Commission suggested a Two Language Formula.

1953: The All-India Language Development Conference decided that tribal languages were acceptable media for primary schools.

1954: The Congress Working Committee agreed that the use of tribal languages was acceptable in primary schools.

1956: The CABE suggested the Three-Language Formula. The Second Five-Year Plan included provision for making textbooks in minority languages.

1961: The Conference of Chief Ministers of various states approved a simplified Three-Language Formula with the purpose to promote national integration and equalise the burden of learning languages on children in Hindi and non-Hindi speaking areas.

1964–1966: The Education Commission emphasised the role of mother tongue education for the massive resurgence of national life, the development of indigenous languages, the achievement of industrialisation and modernisation goals through wider dissemination of science and scientific outlook and the release of original, creative thinking necessary for national development. The Education Commission issued a Modified 3-Language Formula.

1968: The National Policy on Education urged implementation of the 3-Language Formula.

1986: The National Policy on Education (paragraph 4.8) states:

> Some minority groups are educationally deprived or backward. Greater attention will be paid to the education of these groups in the interest of equality and social justice. This will naturally include the constitutional guarantees given to them to establish and administer their own educational institutions, and protection to their languages and culture. Simultaneously, objectivity will be reflected in the preparation of textbooks and in all school activities, and all possible measure will be taken to promote an integration based on appreciation of common national goals and ideals, in conformity with the core curriculum.

Sources: Compiled from Dua (1986); Khubchandani (1981, 2001); Ekbote (1984); Groff (2013).

Social Justice Policies

India has a long history of putting in place social justice programme. Not only is it the world's longest running and most comprehensive programme, it remains one of the most successful examples of social engineering across the globe (Galanter, 1984; Weiner, 1983; Weisskopf, 2004). A unique feature of this programme is to provide 'minimum guaranteed' representation to historically oppressed and socioeconomically marginalised communities in educational opportunities, government services and legislative bodies. It, thus, means a dignified accommodation into opportunity structures; a powerful instrument of lifting the beneficiary groups from the morass of socioeconomic deprivation; and an effective strategy to counter deeply entrenched discriminatory practices against them. Furthermore, unlike preferential policies elsewhere, India's social justice programme is 'long term, institutionalized and legally sanctified', which shields it from everyday politico-legal contestations and bureaucratic prejudices towards the beneficiary groups.

However, the social justice programme has, ever since its inception, come in for a great deal of criticism on many counts. A serious charge facing the social justice programme is that it is a shorthand for group (caste) based reservation, ignoring individual based deprivation as the basis for selection of beneficiaries. Second, it is a regime of 'exclusive inclusion' as the programme, by design, tends to exclude many deserving members of minority communities whose conditions are even worse than the identified beneficiaries. This issue, in recent years, has been a matter of intense, often polarised, political and public debates. The ensuing discussion, though briefly and also at the risk of slight repetition, attempts to capture the trajectories of the demands for and debates around inclusion of disadvantaged minorities into India's social justice programme. It also analyses the patterns of response of the Indian state to such demands.

Historically, the practice of group-specific preferential policies in India can be traced back to the colonial times. While no specific rights were granted to any specific communities, the colonial regime in the early twentieth century marked out definite communities as deserving special treatment. These communities included 'depressed classes', to be designated later as the Scheduled Castes (SCs) and Scheduled Tribes (STs) and religious minorities. The colonial regime applied these (preferential) policies in various fields such as public employment and political representative bodies in order to balance the interests of communities.[33]

As India embarked on framing the Constitution (the proceedings of which began on 9 December 1946) the ideas and issues of social justice came up for intense discussions in the Constituent Assembly (CA). The claims for social justice in the CA were broadly made on two grounds—diversity and backwardness. The diversity logic was largely invoked and argued to be desirable by the representatives of religious minorities. The argument, in short, was that giving representation to every community in the structures of opportunities would make democracy more representative and inclusive. But this argument did not cut much ice with most members of the CA. Eventually, the makers of the Indian Constitution rejected 'diversity' as legitimate ground as in their vision public policymaking based on ascriptively defined groups such as religion would not only undermine the commitment to secularism; the principles of equality and justice would also be deeply compromised (Bajpai, 2000, 2011; Jha, 2003). Hence religious minorities were not to be part of and benefiting from the social justice programme.

On the other hand, 'backwardness' struck a strong chord amongst the CA members as the legitimate ground for special measures. It was argued that historically disadvantaged groups such as the SCs and STs had so far not been able to participate in the opportunities available to the wider society primarily because of their backwardness. Therefore, to ensure their participation in public spheres for the sake of deepening and strengthening of democracy they needed special measures though for a short period of time (10 years). It is, nevertheless, important

[33] For example, the colonial state under constitutional reforms in 1909 granted separate electorate to Muslims. The Government of India Acts of 1919 and 1935 extended these provisions to Sikhs, Indian Christians and a host of other communal and functional groups. In 1925, the colonial government initiated the policy of reserving a certain percentage of direct appointments to government service for Muslims. This was further extended to other communities under the Government of India Act of 1935.

to note that while claims of 'backwardness' put forward by SCs and STs were readily recognised by the CA, similar claims made by other lower castes (just above the line of pollution) remained unresolved due partly to differences amongst the members of CA on the notion of backwardness (Galanter, 1984). It, thus, suggests that who would benefit from the prospective social justice programme did lack coherent principles and sound rationales.

As the CA could not resolve the issues of 'what constitutes backwardness', the problem cropped up early on. In view of the growing demands of inclusion of the lower castes in the social justice programme and policies, the Government of India appointed the Backward Class Commission in 1953 to identify socially and educationally backward classes [as provided in Article 15(4) of the Constitution]. Again, the Commission could only draw up a list of ascriptively defined groups (castes/*jatis*) rather than individuals based on objective criteria who could be identified as 'backward' (Galanter, 1978, 1984; Jenkins, 2000).

For minorities, the appointment of the Commission also opened up a fresh opportunity to put forward their claims for inclusion in the social justice programme along with others (likely to be identified as backward). The Commission received representations from religious groups and organisations. For instance, Muslim organisations in their representation demanded that the Muslim community as a whole should be treated as backward. While the Commission rejected the demand of treating an entire community as a backward class (also see the chapter 'Politics of Minority Accommodation in Postcolonial India') it recognised some groups/sub-groups among them as 'backward classes'.

While the report of the first ever Backward Class Commission was given a quiet burial as it had got mired in controversies, the demands of lower castes (other than SCs) did not die down. The growing political clout of the lower castes over the years led to the appointment of the Second Backward Class Commission in 1977 (popularly known as Mandal Commission after its chairman B.P. Mandal). Like its predecessor, the Mandal Commission too identified a number of individual castes as socially and educationally backward. In justifying 'caste' as the criterion of backwardness, the Second Backward Classes Commission concluded in its report that 'castes are the building bricks of the Hindu social structure [and] in the traditional Indian society … and social backwardness was a direct consequence of caste status' (Report of the Backward Class Commission, 1980, p. 22), although this reasoning was widely contested and criticised (Beteille, 1990).

Nevertheless, the Mandal Commission identified some groups among non-Hindus as socially and educationally backward classes based on the twin criteria: (a) all untouchables converted to non-Hindu religion and (b) such occupational communities known by the name of their traditional hereditary occupation and whose Hindu counterparts were included in the list of Hindu OBCs. The ex-untouchables among non-Hindus, otherwise officially categorised as SCs, were included in the OBC list because, as per the law, the SCs could only be identified among Hindus. Hence, the Mandal Commission chose to stay away from addressing the tension between the 'question of fact' and the 'question of law' (also see the chapter 'Politics of Minority Accommodation in Postcolonial India' and Box 4.4 further). Moreover, the oversimplified criteria used by the Commission for determining OBCs among religious minorities implied not just 'misrecognition' but also 'unrecognition' as proper identification of OBCs among minorities was given a short shrift, leading to the exclusion of many genuinely deserving subgroups among minorities who would otherwise be recognised as 'backward'. This is evident from a much lower share of minorities among OBCs.[34]

[34] As notified by the Ministry of Social Welfare on 13 September 1993, there were 2,159 groups in the central list of OBCs. The religious composition of these groups is as follows: Hindus - 2083, Muslims - 52, Christians - 22 and Sikhs - 02. In the state list, there were a total of 2,332 groups: Hindus - 2123, Muslims - 163, Christian - 38 and Sikhs - 06.

Clearly, while the social justice programme expanded over the years in terms of scope and coverage the inclusion deficits with respect to minorities got only partially corrected. To put it a little differently, social justice gaps remained unplugged even in the era of so-called social justice revolution and hence continued the demand of minorities for greater inclusion in the social justice programme (Alam, 2014; Wright Jr., 1997).

After many years of silence, the Indian state under the Congress-led UPA government responded to such demands by appointing the 'National Commission for Religious and Linguistic Minorities' (NCRLM) in 2004 that submitted its report in 2007. Its mandate included: (a) to suggest criteria for identification of socially and economically backward sections among religious and linguistic minorities; (b) to recommend measures for welfare of socially and economically backward sections among religious and linguistic minorities, including reservation in education and government employment and (c) to suggest the necessary constitutional, legal and administrative modalities required for the implementation of its recommendations.

For an adequate representation of minorities (of Muslims in particular) in the reservation system, NCRLM offered two proposals. One, the entire Muslim community may be declared 'backward' within the meaning of that term in Article 16(4) of the Constitution—notably without qualifying the word 'backward' with the words 'socially' and 'educationally' and that reservation could be given over and above the existing 49.5 per cent. Within this scheme, it suggested 15 per cent reservation for minorities, subdivided into 10 per cent for Muslims and 5 per cent for other minorities. The second proposal is, in fact, placed as an alternative in case there is any difficulty in implementing the first proposal. According to this proposal, subject to minor adjustment inter se in accordance with population of various minorities in various states/UTs, a sub-quota of 8.4 per cent for minorities (internally sub-divided into 6 per cent for Muslims and 2.4 per cent for other minorities) within the 27 per cent OBC quota should be carved out on the ground that minorities account for 8.4 per cent of the total OBC population.

However, both the proposals appeared to be tangled with legal/constitutional problems. As far as the first proposal is concerned, recognising entire the Muslim community as 'backward' for the purpose of reservation involves amendments in the constitution for: (a) extending reservation to Muslims as a 'backward class' and (b) removing the ceiling of 50 per cent. On the second proposal, it has been argued that the inclusion of groups in the category of OBC is based on the twin criteria of 'social' and 'educational' backwardness. As stated earlier, since Indian Muslims comprise a multitude of sub-groups and the fact that some of them are of high social origin, the idea of inclusion of the entire Muslim community is not in the fitness of constitutional provisions. Due to these legal/constitutional difficulties and also because of historically persistent, stronger and, at times, violent resistance to extension of reservation to newer groups in general and to any attempt of making minorities part of the reservation system in particular, the UPA government (2004–2014) developed cold feet. As a result, the recommendations of NCRLM remained unimplemented. Instead, it chose to embark on other measures to address relative backwardness of the religious minorities, Muslims in particular. A detailed discussion of the same is provided in Box 4.5.

Box 4.5: Struggling for Scheduled Caste Status: The Case of Dalit Muslims and Christians

A major reason for the exclusion of minorities from the social justice programme is the wilful denial of the Indian state to recognise deserving members of minority groups as the Scheduled Castes. It is well known that in India that religions other than Hinduism mostly comprise converts who occupied the lowest rungs within the Hindu social system. Theologically, Islam and Christianity profess equality among the believers but the two communities have always been subdivided into caste-like groups as are present among Hindus. Group membership is determined by birth which, in turn, determines other social relations such as marriage, patterns of intermingling, access to places of worship, etc. though with some variations across religions. A large body of ethnographic studies has suggested that the converts of lowest social origin (the Dalits or ex-untouchables, officially known as the Scheduled Castes) who embraced Islam and Christianity in order to escape social discrimination and ostracisation continue to face social disabilities and practice marginal occupations. The Dalit Christians often tend to have separate churches whereas Dalit Muslims are often denied the same burial ground being used by other Muslims. In brief, in spite of the change in their religion, the Dalits belonging to these two communities have experienced no visible change in their social and economic circumstances.

The category of Scheduled Castes, introduced by the British regime in 1935, encompass castes that have historically been oppressed and denied societal, cultural and economic opportunities. The creation of this special category aimed at giving them preferential treatment in educational institutions, government jobs, political representation and in a range of welfare measures undertaken by the government. After independence, while an Order of the President retained the rule that 'no person professing a religion different from Hinduism shall be deemed a member of a Scheduled Caste' it has been amended twice in 1956 and 1990 to include Sikh communities and neo-Buddhists respectively, thus denying the same to members of Muslim and Christian communities.

It has led to movements and litigations. The proponents of the demand for Scheduled Caste status for members of these religious communities have argued that the religion test for inclusion is an outright religion-based discrimination. The courts have so far been reluctant to give legal effect to caste standing among communities professing Islam and Christianity. In the famous Soosai case, the Supreme Court held that 'it is not sufficient to show that the same caste continues after conversion. It is necessary to establish further that the disabilities and handicaps suffered from such caste membership in the social order of its origin—Hinduism—continue in their oppressive severity in the new environment of a different religious community' (Soosai vs. Union of India, 1985).

However, the NCRLM (headed by Justice Ranganath Misra) in its report (2007, p. 154) recommended that 'Para 3 of the Constitution (Scheduled Castes) Order 1950—which originally restricted the Scheduled Caste net to the Hindus and later opened it to Sikhs and Buddhists, thus still excluding from its purview the Muslims, Christians, Jains and Parsis, etc.—should be wholly deleted by appropriate action so as to completely delink the Scheduled Caste status from religion and make the Scheduled Castes' net fully religion-neutral like that of the Scheduled Tribes'. The Central Government is yet to act on this to plug the social justice gaps.

Sources: Deshpande (2008); Galanter (1984); Jenkins (2000).

Affirmative Action Policies

While religious minorities per se were not considered as 'backward' and, therefore, not included in the social justice programme (as discussed in the preceding section), many Congress leaders, Jawaharlal Nehru in particular, were concerned about the poor representation of minorities in public spheres including public employment. Early on (1953), in his letter to chief ministers of the states, Jawaharlal Nehru expressed his concerns as thus:

> In the services, generally speaking, the representation of the minority communities is lessening. In some cases, it is very poor indeed. Looking through the Central Secretariat figures, as well as some others, I am distressed to find that the position is very disadvantageous to them, chiefly to the Muslims and sometimes to others also. In the vast Central Secretariat of Delhi, there are very few Muslims. (Parthasarthy, 1985, p. 376)

But in spite of anxieties about representation of minorities in various democratic institutions and opportunities public policies in the following decades of independence remained indifferent to whether and how far minorities benefited from scores of developmental programmes. Nor did nodal data collecting agencies such as Census of India and National Sample Survey Organization (NSSO) divulge socioeconomic statistics by religious category. Although some micro-level studies carried out in the 1960s and 1970s did point to the relative socioeconomic and educational backwardness facing some minorities, especially Muslims (Sharma, 1978; Sherwani, 1979), they failed to generate sufficient public debates so as to influence public policymaking for attending to issues of educational and economic backwardness faced by members of some, if not all, minority communities.

It was, nevertheless, in 1980 that a major policy shift pertaining to minorities occurred when Indira Gandhi, the then prime minister of India, appointed a High-Power Panel under the chairmanship of Gopal Singh to study the educational and economic plight of the religious minorities. As it was the first government-appointed commission in the post-independent era to look into socioeconomic issues of minorities, elites belonging to minority communities welcomed the government's gesture. But the euphoria died down soon as the government of the day decided to shelve the findings of the report submitted in 1983. However, Rafiq Zakaria, the Member Secretary of the Panel, revealed that:

> [T]he Panel sent out 200 researchers to every state, to collect data on sample survey basis, so as to assess the actual situation in every field. For almost four years they worked, travelled from one place to another. What they gathered proved an eye-opener. On the basis of the facts and figures so collected the Panel prepared a comparative report which sent shock waves through the corridors of South Block. Mrs. [Indira] Gandhi thought it best to shelve its findings. (Zakaria, 1995, p. 163)

Although the findings of the Gopal Singh Committee were not made public, some excerpts were leaked to the media that generated some public debates. But again, they were to be lost in the politics of communalism that ensued in subsequent years. Nevertheless, the government announced a variety of schemes for the welfare of minorities under the Prime Minister's 15-Point Programme. A deeper look at it would, however, suggest that this remarkable policy turn had taken place in an interesting political context. It was a time when the political hegemony of the Congress Party had been challenged in many states. As a result, it was losing power in one state after another. There were many reasons for it. But one of the reasons was dwindling support of minorities to the Congress. For instance, Rudolph and Rudolph (1987) in their study observed that the Congress had received a lower percentage of votes in two consecutive elections in the years 1977 and 1980 in the 207 parliamentary constituencies that had a Muslim population of 10 per cent or more. Hence, the appointment of the Gopal Singh Commission by the Congress Party, in large part, was an attempt to bring the minorities back into its fold.

Further, political fragmentation due mainly to the rise of political formations of secular orientation in many crucial states in the 1990s marked a new phase from the point of view of policy focus on minorities. With the rise of newly formed secular political formations in the 1990s in several states the sands of electoral support of minorities, Muslim minorities in particular, to the Congress Party began to shift and slide drastically. Having lost its critical support base, the Congress Party performed miserably in 1996 parliamentary elections and remained out of power until 2004. As soon as the Congress-led alliance of UPA came to power in 2004, it announced in its Common Minimum Programme (CMP), among other things, that, 'The UPA will establish a National Commission to see how best the welfare of socially and economically backward section among religious and linguistic minorities, including reservation in education and employment, is enhanced.' Interestingly enough, the UPA government following up on this item of CMP actually constituted two Commissions (instead of one) and almost around the same time.

The Prime Minister's High-Power Panel, popularly known as Sachar Committee[35] and the NCRLM[36] analysed a wealth of empirical data pertaining to socioeconomic attainment of socioreligious communities and also recommended a variety of policy measures (including reservation as discussed in the preceding section). The findings of these two commissions, of the former in particular, brought to the fore that Muslims, if not all religious minorities, were faced with acute level of marginalisation, deprivation and exclusion across dimensions—social, educational, economic, political and so on (Basant, 2007; Basant and Shariff, 2010; Robinson, 2007; Shah, 2007).

In the economic sphere, the Sachar Committee Report (SCR) unambiguously underscored the fact that the Muslims as a minority group experienced a higher incidence of poverty and unemployment than the national average. There were among them a disproportionately large proportion of workers who were either self-employed (mostly in petty business and street vending) or were casual workers. Relative to other socioreligious communities, they were least likely to have access to jobs in the formal sector—both government and private (Table 4.1).

In the sphere of education, Muslims were found to have higher illiteracy and lower school attendance rates than the national average. The proportion of graduates among them was found to be the least.

[35] The mandate given to the committee broadly included: (a) to 'obtain relevant information from departments/agencies of Central & State Governments and also conduct an intensive literature survey to identify published data, articles and research on relative social, economic and educational statistics of Muslims in India at the State, regional and district levels...', (b) to 'consolidate, collate and analyse the above information/literature to identify areas of intervention by Government to address relevant issues relating to the social, economic and educational status of the Muslim community'. Also see Notification No. 850/3/C/3/05 – Pol. Government of India, New Delhi.

[36] The NCRLM was primarily mandated to find out solutions to socioeconomic problems faced by the Muslim community. Its mandate included: (a) suggest criteria for identification of socially and economically backward sections among religious and linguistic minorities; (b) recommend measures for welfare of socially and economically backward sections among religious and linguistic minorities, including reservation in education and government employment and (c) to suggest the necessary constitutional, legal and administrative modalities required for the implementation of its recommendations.

Worse still, the educational status of Muslims in many situations was discovered to have slipped down the level of SCs/STs, the most deprived communities of the country. The report also revealed some disturbing aspects of the developmental processes. It showed that the settlements predominantly inhabited by Muslims were marked by acute deficits of basic amenities and public services—approach roads, banks and post offices and educational and medical facilities—all of them meant to be provided universally. To add to this, not only did Muslims appear to have poor access to bank credit, their habitations were often marked out by banks as 'red zones'. This grim story of deprivation simply pointed to the fact that the developmental processes during the past six decades had altogether bypassed the Muslim minorities.

Table 4.1: Educational and Economic Status of Muslims (2004–2005)

Indicators	*All*	*Hindu*	*Muslim*
Educational			
Literacy rate (aged 7 years and above)	64.8	65.1	59.1
Proportion of children (aged 6–14) attending educational institutions	85.3	86.1	79.5
Proportion of children (aged 15–19) attending educational institutions	46.0	46.9	36.1
Proportion of graduates and above (20 years and above)	7.0	6.5	3.0
Economic			
Proportion of main workers	48.1	49.1	42.2
Proportion of marginal workers	13.0	13.5	10.4
Proportion of non-workers	38.9	37.5	47.5
Proportion of rural workers engaged in informal sector	88.5	87.7	94.2
Proportion of urban workers engaged in informal sector	79.1	76.9	92.1
Proportion of rural workers engaged in formal sector	11.5	12.3	5.8

Indicators	*All*	*Hindu*	*Muslim*
Proportion of urban workers engaged in formal sector	20.9	23.1	7.9
Proportion of regular salaried workers in Government sector	34.2	35.3	23.7
Proportion of regular salaried workers in Public/Private ltd.	13.1	13.9	6.5
Monthly per capita expenditure (current prices)			
MPCE (Urban)	1,105	1,139	804
MPCE (Rural)	579	568	553
Incidence of poverty			
Poverty ratio (Urban)	29	27	44
Poverty ratio (Rural)	28	28	33

Notes: MPCE refers to monthly per capita expenditure.
Source: Based on Sachar Committee Report (2006).

While Muslims, on the whole, have been on the margin across dimensions, it is important to discuss, albeit briefly, the nature and patterns of their marginalisation and exclusion. First and foremost, there are 'geographies of exclusion'. The aggregate picture often masks regional contrasts of achievements and deficits, and, therefore, is misleading. For instance, Muslims living in the four southern states (Andhra Pradesh, Karnataka, Kerala and Tamil Nadu) appear to have done quite well on many crucial indicators of human and social development as compared to their counterpart living in other parts of the country. Relatively better socioeconomic conditions enjoyed by Muslims in the southern states could be attributed to a complex mix of factors. These include, but are not limited to, absence of communal violence and religion-based political mobilisation; long history of backward class movements for socioeconomic empowerment; greater share of Muslims in the affirmative action programme; and, of course, better record of overall governance (Basant and Shariff, 2010; Robinson, 2005; Shariff and Razzack, 2006).

Similarly, there are stark rural–urban differences in the levels and degrees of deprivation. Relative to rural Muslims, those living in urban areas have less access to public services. There are many reasons for it. In part, it is, as suggested by some scholars, an outcome of frequent communal riots in many cities that have tended to sweep Muslims to particular type of neighbourhoods, often labelled as 'Muslim ghettos' (Gayer and Jafferlot, 2012). Across the globe, such kind of ethnically bounded socio-spatial formations are negatively stereotyped and, therefore, often marked by inadequate infrastructure facilities as well as various sorts of opportunities. Part of it is also due to huge 'class' difference between Muslims and other communities in urban centres, compared to rural areas. In urban areas, public services are markedly different in terms of neighbourhood status (lower class/middle class). It is well known that Muslims took more time to join modern education introduced by the British in the first half of the nineteenth century. As a result, they remained tied to their traditional occupations and saw little, if any, economic mobility which was taking place in towns and cities (Alam, 2012). Scarcely had the situation begun to improve by the early twentieth century, the partition of the country (in 1947) served a heavy blow as it caused a flight of the educated and articulate Muslim middle class mostly from towns and cities, further widening the class gaps between them and the rest (Imam, 1978).

An equally important dimension linked to developmental deficits among Muslims is their sociology—internal differentiations and inner contradictions. In much contrast to the popular perceptions, the 'Muslim Social' is far more complicated than other communities as Muslims as a community consists of groups drawn from multiple racial stocks, social origins and occupational practices. Scholars have pointed out that while social stratification and rules of social interactions among Muslims might be less rigid than among Hindus, the fact remains that in spite of Islam's emphasis on equality and universal brotherhood, caste-like formations and practices are present among them (Muslims) though with important regional variations (Ahmad, 1978; Ahmad and Chakravarti, 1981). As Muslims are a conglomeration of varied racial, ethnic and occupational groups—each of which historically having differential access to societal resources, opportunities and power—their socioeconomic conditions are bound to vary in accord with their lineage, ethnicity and traditional occupations. This is also confirmed by the SCR (2006) which, though in a limited way, found Muslims of lower social origin (the *Ajlafs*) way behind those of higher social origin (the *Ashrafs*) in terms of socioeconomic attainment.[37]

The Muslim communities are also marked by greater gender differentials in socioeconomic achievement. Undeniably, Indian women across religious and social locations are less likely than men to have access to educational and economic opportunities, but Muslim women have appeared to be the worst. Not only are Muslim women faced with opportunity deprivation relative to Muslim men, they have also fallen far behind their counterpart belonging to other religions (Hasan and Menon, 2004; Sachar, 2006). It, thus, suggests that Muslim women are doubly disadvantaged—as women and as Muslim. Exclusion of Muslim women from societal opportunities, educational and economic in particular, has severely affected overall socioeconomic standing as well as status of the community.

In sum, relative developmental deficits among Muslims are not entirely an outcome of extraneous factors such as their status as a suspicious minority and overt or covert discrimination against them by the state and its agencies but also caused by factors that are internal to them as a collectivity. Nevertheless, the findings of SCR (2006) not

---

[37] Of late, sociology of Muslims has drawn increasing attention of many scholars, and as a result there has appeared a large body of literature on social differentiation among Muslims and its association with occupational mobility, social modernisation and general social well-being. See for example, Ahmad (1978), Ali (2002), Mondal (2003), Sikand (2004).

only dismantled the myth of appeasement of Muslims that has been created and sustained by the right-wing forces but also helped create a context of policy focus and priorities for the community.

Following up on the recommendations of SCR, the older version of PM's 15-Point Programme for the welfare of minorities announced in 1983 was revamped and recast in 2006. The following constituted the major objectives of the programme: (a) enhancing opportunities for education; (b) ensuring an equitable share for minorities in economic activities and employment; (c) improving the conditions of living of minorities by ensuring an appropriate share for them in infrastructure development schemes and (d) prevention and control of communal disharmony and violence. In the light of these objectives, the government initiated many schemes and programmes being implemented by various ministries/departments.

Of course, crafting and putting in place policies aimed especially at plugging developmental deficits facing minorities is an important step. But equally, if not more, important is how such policies get implemented on the ground and do the benefits reach those for whom they are meant. Most often, such policies turn out to be mere political populism or tokenism in which case minorities may eventually end up losing more than gaining as group-specific policies, irrespective of how they work, often generate backlash from the non-beneficiary groups. Keeping this in view, the ensuing discussion attempts to review the performance of some important schemes/programmes undertaken for the welfare and empowerment of disadvantaged minorities.

Access to Educational Opportunities

Given the glaring educational deficit among some minorities, as discussed earlier, the government has initiated a number of schemes aimed at improving their access to and participation in educational opportunities. These include the construction of new schools and investment in improving educational infrastructure in minority concentrated localities/areas/settlements; scholarship for meritorious minority students at school/college/university levels; free coaching for competitive examinations; and modernisation of madrasas. Besides, a scheme of interest subsidy on educational loan for studying overseas has also been initiated. Apparently, these schemes are quite promising in terms of making an impact on educational problems faced by the disadvantaged students belonging particularly to minority communities. For example, the scholarship schemes are not only likely to attract students to get into educational opportunities but also help reduce higher incidence of dropout observed among them. Similarly, the scheme of free (high quality) coaching may significantly help minority students to prepare themselves for competitive examinations, thereby getting access to socially prestigious and economically valued jobs.

How do these schemes perform? As seen in Table 4.2, efforts are made towards addressing the deficiency of schooling opportunities in the minority concentrated areas by way of opening up new schools. Although, the targets between the financial years 2006–2007 and 2013–2014 (a period of seven years) have been smaller than

Table 4.2: New Schools Opened and Constructed in Districts with Substantial Minority Population: All India—2006–2007 to 2013–2014

New Schools Opened	*Target*	*Achievement*	*Rate of Achievement (%)*
Primary School	23,404	21,486	91.8
Upper Primary School	13,902	11,871	85.3
Schools Constructed			
Primary school	21,726	15,939	73.3
Upper Primary Schools	10,326	8,151	78.9

Source: Annual Reports (2006–2007, 2013–2014), Ministry of Minority Affairs, Government of India.

the requirement, the achievement rates against the targets are, nevertheless, impressive (more than 75 per cent) at the national level. There are, of course, state-wide variations. But it is interesting to note that the schemes of opening and constructing new schools seem to be doing well across the states. For example, the achievement rate in many bigger states such as Assam, Bihar, Maharashtra, Uttar Pradesh and West Bengal that have sizeable minority populations and minorities being educationally more disadvantaged than others, the achievement rates have been either at par with or above the national average.

A look at the scholarship programme suggests that over the years both the number of scholarships and amount sanctioned for the same, increased year after year in the period between 2008–2009 and 2013–2014. In the beginning, the targets were too small—300,000 and 170,000 for pre- and post-matric scholarship respectively—but increased manifold in the subsequent years (Table 4.3). Interestingly,

Table 4.3: Scholarships to Students Belonging to Minority Communities: All India

Pre-matric Scholarship	*2008–2009*	*2009–2010*	*2010–2011*	*2011–2012*	*2012–2013*	*2013–2014*
No. of scholarship (in '000)	300	1,500	2,000	3,400	4,000	4,000
Amount sanctioned (in ₹ crore)	62	203	446	615	786	964
Post-matric scholarship						
No. of scholarship (in '000)	170	364	526	700	756	890
Amount sanctioned (in ₹ crore)	71	149	229	363	326	515

Notes: (a) Figures are rounded off; (b) one crore (INR) equals to 10 million.
Sources: Annual Reports (2008–2009, 2009–2010, 2010–2011, 2011–2012, 2012–2013, 2013–2014), Ministry of Minority Affairs, Government of India.

at the national level the scholarship programmes are actually marked by overachievement (Kundu, 2014), suggesting that more scholarships were distributed than actually targeted. Put simply, the scholarship schemes are quite popular and benefiting the students of minority communities in a big way.

The free coaching and allied schemes aimed at empowering the minority communities, enhancing their skills and capabilities to make them employable in industries, services or getting admission in universities/technical institutions have been expanding over the years both in terms of the number of beneficiaries and amount sanctioned for the scheme. As can be seen in Table 4.4 there has been a significant increase in the amount disbursed for these schemes. From a mere 0.41 crore in the beginning in 2006–2007, the amount disbursed has increased to 23.7 crores in 2013–2014. On the other hand, the number of beneficiary students has increased from less than a 1,000 in 2006–2007 to about 10,000 in 2013–2014. Similarly, the average cost of providing coaching and allied services per student at the national level was ₹ 6,000 in 2006–2007 which went up to ₹ 23,671 in 2013–2014. Among the states, Uttar Pradesh, Delhi and Andhra Pradesh have been major beneficiaries of this scheme.

Table 4.4: Free Coaching and Allied Schemes for the Candidates Belonging to Minority Communities

Year	*No. of Students Benefited*	*Amount Sanctioned (in ₹ crore)*
2006–2007	690	0.414
2007–2008	4,097	5.742
2008–2009	5,522	7.300
2009–2010	5,532	11.219
2010–2011	4,845	14.373
2011–2012	7,880	15.980
2012–2013	6,716	13.997
2013–2014	9,997	23.664

Note: One crore (INR) equals to 10 million.
Source: Annual Report, respective years, Ministry of Minority Affairs, Government of India.

While this particular scheme appears to be getting popular, many concerns with regard to its actual impact remain. First, there is hardly any audit done about the success of the students receiving coaching. Second, the selection of the coaching centres for providing coaching has often been without much screening and probably many relevant points may not have been taken into account. For this scheme to make a greater impact, it is important that coaching centres are selected where the students can also get residential/hostel facilities so that their precious time is not lost in commuting to these centres. Finally, evaluation of the coaching centres and success of the candidates must be done regularly for providing financial assistance to coaching centres otherwise the scheme will become a money minting business for the coaching centres (Kundu, 2014).

Modernisation of the madrasa (Islamic educational institutions) is also part of the educational empowerment policy package for Muslim minorities as many Muslim children do attend religious seminaries. The intended aim of this scheme is to strengthen the teaching of mathematics and science and to provide training to work with computers and the digital economy. Given the excessive focus of madrasa curricula on the study of religious texts and lower probability of those graduating from a madrasa in finding jobs in the modern labour market, this particular scheme has been appreciated by many.[38]

Available data seem to show a significant increase in the amount sanctioned by the Central Government for this scheme. The amount sanctioned increased from ₹42.52 crore in 2009–2010 to ₹139.53 crore in 2011–2012. The number of madrasas benefitting from the scheme has gone up from 1,760 in 2009–2010 to 5,934 in 2011–2012. During the same period, the financial support to teachers from the

[38] However, a section of *ulema* (religious teachers/preachers/leaders) has been suspicious of this scheme, and, therefore, are opposed to it. In their view, this scheme is a deliberate attempt of the government to get into the affairs of their educational institutions.

modernisation grants increased from 4,713 to 14,412 teachers. The popularity of this scheme grew across states during this period. For instance, in 2009–2010 only Uttar Pradesh, Tripura, Madhya Pradesh, Jharkhand and Chandigarh used the scheme, but in 2010–2011 the number of states using this went up to 12. In 2013–2014, a total ₹ 182.73 crore was released for 14,859 madrasas involving 35,376 teachers. The figures thus show that modernisation of madrasa scheme is benefiting quite a large number of institutions and individuals associated with them.

Multi-sectoral Development Programme

As the SCR (2006) pointed out the glaring lack of basic amenities in minority concentrated pockets/spaces, the government launched an umbrella programme called Multi-sectoral Development Programme (MsDP) in 2008–2009 with an aim to plug developmental deficits in minority concentrated areas. The projects taken up under MsDP pertain to the provision of better infrastructure for education, skill development, health, sanitation, pucca (cemented) housing, roads, drinking water, besides schemes for creating income generating opportunities.

Given the scale and coverage of this programme, it is described as the largest ever programme for the development of minorities since independence. But unfortunately, this programme is marked by tardy implementation. For example, in the Eleventh Five-Year Plan only 69 per cent of the physical target of drinking water supply could be completed. The achievement was as low as 47 per cent in construction and upgradation of Industrial Training Institutes (ITIs) and about 58 per cent on solar lantern distribution. The achievement rate in construction of hostels was 71 per cent.

Moreover, some independent research (for example, Khan and Parvati, 2013) has brought to the fore many concerns with regard to 'coverage', 'content' and 'implementation' of the programme. In terms of coverage, the minority concentrated districts (MCDs) as defined by the government[39] contained only 37 per cent of the minority population. Thus, majority of minorities lived outside the MCDs. On the 'content' problem, the schemes under MsDP are very few. These schemes basically include providing houses to poor, construction of additional classrooms, skill development initiatives, etc. On the 'implementation' front, there were no clear guidelines as to the selection of activities and where in the selected districts activities were to be carried out. As a result, in many instances funds were diverted and the activities being undertaken in ways that would end up benefiting non-minority population.

Under UPA II, efforts were made to address many of the key concerns about the working of MsDP. Acknowledging that the district is too big a unit for planning, the government has now switched to sub-district as a unit of planning, funding and implementation of projects. A total of 710 minority concentration blocks (with 25 per cent or more minority population) in 155 backward districts have been identified. Also, the new guidelines suggest that in selected sub-districts (blocks) the villages having higher minority population would be given priority for creation of village level infrastructure/ assets. Thus, now the need is to enlarge the bouquet of schemes and remove the implementation bottlenecks such as the indifferent attitude of local authorities, inadequate planning capacity at the district level, multiple layers of authorities for planning and approval of projects and non-submission of the detailed project plan by the state governments for allocation of funds.

Access to Financial Credit

Among the members of minority communities, a major obstacle towards economic progress is the lack of working capital and poor access to institutional credit. As the minority concentrated areas are

[39] The MCDs included districts having a 25 per cent or more share of the minority population.

often labelled by commercial banks as 'red zones', the government has taken multiple initiatives for financial inclusion of minority communities. The creation of National Minorities Development and Finance Corporation (NMDFC) is an important step in this direction. The main mandate of NMDFC is to provide concessional loans to minorities so as to help them set up or scale up business or enterprises.

Over the years, the amount disbursed as credit by NMDFC has increased though not to the extent expected. At the national level, as per the statistics provided by Ministry of Minority Affairs (MoMA), the amount disbursed increased from ₹10 crore in 2005–2006 to 186.7 crore in 2012–2013, but declined to 122.96 crores in 2013–2014. Similarly, the number of beneficiaries increased manifold—from 10,893 in 2005–2006 to 82,978 in 2012–2013, but declined to 54,648 in 2013–2014. The amount disbursed under term loan by NMDFC has also shown a modest increase—from ₹ 130.9 crore in 2006–2007 to ₹184.4 crore in 2012–2013.

Two key concerns emerge from the data available. One, given the size of population and expanse and depth of deprivation among minorities, especially among the Muslims, the amount disbursed as credit and term loan remains far from adequate to financially empower the minority communities. Second, NMDFC in many states has turned irrelevant as it did not disburse any loan in the period between 2007–2008 and 2012–2013. Besides NMDFC, the PM's 15-Point Programme also stressed the need for a certain share of priority sector lending for minorities. The amount disbursed to minorities under priority sector lending increased from ₹ 58,663 crore in 2007–2008 to ₹ 1,64,748 crore in 2011–2012—almost three times increase in four years. The achievement rate against the targets at the national level has also been satisfactory (above 85 per cent). However, a closer examination of figures suggests that the share of credit lent to minorities under priority sector lending has ranged between 7.5 per cent in 2006–2007 to 11.3 per cent in 2012–2013.

This is much lower than the percentage of minority population in the country.

Notwithstanding the lower share of minorities in credit lending by commercial banks, there are glaring state-level variations. It can be noticed that both the target and achievements in states (with higher concentration of Muslims) have been very low. For instance, both the targeted and utilised amounts were very low in Uttar Pradesh. The achievements in Assam, Bihar, West Bengal, and Maharashtra have been relatively lower (less than the target) compared to other states. Up until recently (2014), most of these states were ruled by parties that claimed to be most concerned about the condition of minorities. Many factors account for relatively low success of schemes associated with financial credit. The first is the governmental apathy which is clearly visible in earmarking funds for disbursing financial credits. While reasons for it are not known, it can be surmised that providing financial credit at subsidised interest rates does not square with the neo-liberal economic policy framework. The second important factor is bureaucratic hurdle. Even if fund for credit lending, no matter how tiny it may be, is available, gaining access to financial credit is full of physical and mental harassment as it involves endless paper chase. The third factor is the relative lack of awareness about the schemes especially among the poor most of whom belong to Muslim minorities. This explains why most of the credit meant for minorities has been cornered by those relatively advanced and well off.[40]

It is, thus, clear that while there are many well-meaning schemes aimed at improving conditions of disadvantaged minorities, many challenges lie ahead. The first set of challenge relates to efficacy. There is an urgent need to remove the obstacles to better implementation of

---

[40] For example, while Muslims account for over two-thirds of population of religious minorities, they could get only 44 per cent of primary sector lending as against Sikhs (24.5 per cent) and Christians (21.8 per cent) in 2013–2014. Also see Kundu (2014).

the schemes so that the gap between the political promises/rhetoric for minority development and effective benefits to minorities from the schemes is minimised, if not completely eliminated. The second set of challenges relates to acquiring sociopolitical legitimacy. Schemes targeting specific groups become successful when they enjoy acceptance of the wider society and political actors across the ideological spectrum. In absence of such legitimacy group specific schemes and programmes are likely to generate communally polarised mobilisation and political backlash. As elsewhere, minority specific schemes in India are also seen as undue policy favour and therefore disliked by many. There is, thus, a need for making conscious efforts to spread the narrative that decent socioeconomic conditions experienced by minorities are actually beneficial to the wider society in many ways.

The Upshot: Whither Minorities Policies?

It is rather common for minority groups to feel that the issues faced by them are either ignored or not adequately attended to by the state; that they are denied access to opportunities that may be available to the members of the wider society. There exists, therefore, the tendency among minorities of making exaggerated claims and pressing hard for more access to and participation in the structures of opportunities. The discussion presented in this chapter demonstrates how India has responded to growing socioeconomic inequalities between the majority and minority communities and has used a variety of affirmative measures as an important lever of inclusion of disadvantaged minorities.

India has chosen multiple administrative and policy pathways—ranging from recognising and promoting cultural diversity in public spaces to supporting minority specific educational institutions; from recognising many sub-groups among them as 'backward' (so as to enable them to benefit from the social justice programme) to putting in place a variety of welfare schemes. There are at least three policy aspects that possibly make India a paradigm, if not an exceptional case, of accommodation of minority claims and aspirations when we look at how nations across the globe have tried to deal with the minority question. First and foremost, what minorities must possess and/or what cannot be taken away from them is embedded in the Indian constitution. It is not the case in many democratic pluralistic nations. Second, the template of India's minority policies is too broad as compared to many pluralistic nations. It goes far beyond merely recognising minorities and their religious/cultural traditions, values and practices. Third, India's minority policies combine both institutional and administrative approaches and involve multi-layered and multi-pronged strategies. This is, again, in sharp contrast to other democracies where minority-oriented policies operate in an institutional vacuum. They are not only *ad hoc* in nature but also quite localised in design and implementation.

Though laudable in many respects, India's minority policies bear no unblemished record. Despite many positive steps taken and important advances made in the last seven decades, cultural spaces have seen constant erasure of symbols, icons and cultural practices associated with minorities. Educational spaces remain far from addressing important concerns of minorities. While there are scores of programmes and schemes aimed at improving the everyday life of disadvantaged minorities most of them suffer from inadequate allocation of funds and tardy implementation. As a result, the gains stemming from such schemes have been quite limited. In a sense, efforts made so far have not gone well beyond what may be called 'politically expedient tokenism or symbolism'.

It is important to note that while tokenistic policies may satisfy the demand for state response in public discourse, they do little for the empowerment of minorities on the ground. More often than not, policies undertaken merely with a view to gain electoral support of minorities or for the sake of satisfying demands in public discourse rather than as the embodiment of national commitment tend to be betrayal as they end up causing more harm than good in more ways than one. For one thing, minority specific policies in absence of wider political consensus often give rise to the notion of 'minority appeasement' which, in turn, fuels the political and public debates that contribute to political mobilisation along ethno-majoritarian line seeking to project minorities being favoured at the expense of the majority community (Sheth, 2000). India's minority policies seem to be grappling with this phenomenon. In recent years, the rants against the so-called 'policy favour' to minorities have risen to spectacular prominence. This is not to say that issues specific to minorities and the manner in which they have been handled by parties in power have not played a significant role in shaping the political contours in the postcolonial era but political mobilisation along ethno-majoritarian line has never been so deep and spectacular as it has been since the last decade (2004–2014) that marked significant policy shift associated with minorities.

As shown in this chapter, India's minorities, under the changed political circumstances powered by majoritarian impulse, have begun to experience a situation that is unsettling and unnerving for them. Governmental interference in religio-cultural affairs of minorities, the boundaries of which have been jealously guarded by them, has increased considerably. There are attempts of sanitising public spaces by expunging markers of cultural pluralism. Many minority-specific welfare or ameliorative schemes have landed on the chopping board.[41] For the minorities, and also for a section of the wider society, government actions of such character are deeply disturbing and worrisome. The worry is less because of a few actions of governments (both central and state governments) targeting minorities. It is more because of the feeling that the recent majoritarian turn of the polity entails grave implications for the values (such as syncretism,

[41] For instance, while the targets for scholarships have remained unchanged since 2014, the actual delivery appears to have witnessed a rapid decline in both numerical and financial terms (Bhatnagar, 2018).

secularism and sociocultural pluralism) for which India has been known to the world for ages.

In this context, the question of prime importance is: Has India entered the phase of serious retreat from the policy of 'accommodation'? Or, should the unfolding sociopolitical situation that seeks to reject any policy initiative aimed at inclusion of minorities in various opportunities be merely seen as a blip? Is India headed for ceasing to be a model for the world to emulate or look forward to as to how minorities may be made to feel at home and taken care of?

On the face of it, recent sociopolitical development seems to cast deep shadows on the 'accommodation' approach. Yet, there are reasons to be optimistic. For one thing, the politics of populism is often short-lived. Beyond the realms of political rhetoric and mobilisation, there is a realisation that accommodation of demands and fulfilment of aspirations of minorities, to the extent possible, is good for the nation and its democratic polity. The ongoing developmental processes will remain incomplete unless minorities, who make up a little less than one-fifth of the nation's population, become active participants therein. Nor can India's democratic polity afford deep alienation of minorities. This explains, in part, why a change in the political regime has not resulted in a complete reversal of policies specific to minorities. There is and will remain some degrees of resistance to policies benefiting minorities. But what is unique about India is that its lived social space marked by people belonging to diverse religious faiths or persuasions living cheek by jowl and mutual interdependence has produced a critical mass of public that not only abhors religious extremism and religion based oppression and discrimination but is also supportive of affirmative/ameliorative policies for minorities. Furthermore, it is this critical mass of public that helps, more than the constitutional/legal safeguards available to minorities, keep anti-minority tendencies in check whenever they tend to cross the limit or spin out of control.

To conclude then, India's policy initiative for minorities, with all its imperfections and pitfalls, is an important lever of inclusion and also serves as a valuable guide to pluralistic nations as to how to accommodate claims and aspirations of minorities.

Chapter 5

Conclusion: Learning from India

In Chapter 1 we had invited scholars and policymakers from across the world to study India if they wanted to learn how to respond to minority claims in plural democracies. We had stated that India has a rich history of dealing with such claims and that it offered a range of responses for study, which were both innovative and appropriate for the task of building democratic states. In the previous chapters we had argued that India sought to give minorities a sense of equal citizenship to build a nation that was beautifully captured by Nehru's powerful slogan of 'unity in diversity'. This was India's aspiration. These minority claims that were made could be placed along two axes: their cultural distinctiveness that was valuable because of our commitment to cultural diversity and their socioeconomic disadvantage and backwardness that had to be addressed because of our commitment to social justice. Along each axis, arrangements had to be made to accommodate these claims. To do so, the Indian state enacted specific laws, established dedicated institutions, formulated special policies and encouraged a public discourse that sought to give minorities the feeling that their claims would be attended to and that their presence in the public realm was being regarded as 'normal' and not exceptional. This book has sought to show how in each of these four areas there are lessons to be learnt from the Indian story.

This is not to suggest that the narrative is one of only achievements. There have been many advances in these 70 odd years but there have also been some reverses and pushbacks. For example, the granting of special privileges to minorities because of their claim of cultural distinctiveness, produced a backlash that has resulted in a politics that saw such policies as minority appeasement. Further, if opportunities, through quotas, were being offered to the minorities in educational institutions and in government employment—to increase their presence in the public realm and to reduce the structural asymmetries they experience—this was soon met by opposition from groups belonging to the majority who felt they would suffer and be excluded by these policies. The India story shows that while it was a democracy that produced such enlightened policies, it was also the same democracy that produced the adversarial politics that followed. Our book has documented these achievements and retreats.

Before we set out our summary review of this exercise of minority accommodation, it is important for us to accept that it is possible to learn from both India's successes and failures. This statement, a truism, has become necessary because the present period of assertive majoritarianism in India has caused many to wonder if there are any lessons at all that the world can draw from India. Cynics wonder how has the growth, in spite of several decades of the steady advancement of minority rights, been so fragile that India has, so easily, entered a period of regress. Why, they ask, do minorities, especially Muslims and Christians, feel that their presence in the public realm can only be on the sufferance of the majority? In recent years, particularly since 2014, we have experienced a politics of muscular majoritarianism, where lynchings of individuals from the minority community have taken place, where places of worship have been set on fire, where there are restrictions on the type of food that can be consumed, where there is hostility to interreligious marriages, where there is a concerted attempt to remove the symbols of the minority from public places such as the names of towns and where history textbooks are being rewritten to present historical figures from the minority community as being responsible for the dark deeds in Indian history. These are challenges that Indian democracy will have to face as it navigates its way into a plural future. This book is a small contribution to this project of strengthening plural democracies and should be seen as speaking not just to the contemporary politics of India but also to the contemporary politics of other democracies such as Hungary, the US, Brazil, Turkey, Indonesia and the many countries of Europe, that are also experiencing majoritarian and populist politics. Let us now list some lessons from the India story.

The first important learning is to acknowledge, as a positive feature, the fact that we live in a plural society.[1] This acknowledgement is important to combat a viewpoint that the minorities are present in society because of the mercy of the majority and not because they have rights. It is necessary to recognise that all societies, even those that were hitherto homogenous such as the Nordic countries, are today plural societies. These plural populations have emerged because of multiple factors that range from their colonial histories (Rodríguez, 2018), to the migration of people that follows displacement because of war, to mobility because of the economic need of both migrant and the host country (Grant, 2018). The political landscape that has emerged is a plural landscape where minority groups make demands for recognition, for rights and resources, especially since many of them are now second and third generation citizens.

Such demands must be conceded not just by the political class, that does so sometimes grudgingly, but also by the general population that has to adjust to this new demographic plurality. In the absence of such acceptance by the general population we get instances of pathological violence against minority communities such as was recently experienced by New Zealand on 15 March 2019 when a shooter killed 50 persons during Friday prayers in a mosque (*The New York Times*, 2019). Attacks against mosques are being witnessed in many countries across the world as are attacks against churches in places such as Pakistan and frequently in Egypt against the Coptic Christian minority (*The Guardian*, 2018). These tell us that societies

[1] See footnote 25 in Chapter 1 on Rawls's observation on 'pluralism' in his book *Political Liberalism* (1993).

will have to endure such pathologies unless the general population also accepts the reality of plurality where difference in lifestyle, worship and cultural practices are accepted (Sayeed, 2018). In these majoritarian constructions 'the other' is seen as an adversarial other who must be suppressed and sometimes even eliminated [*History.com* (n.d.); Britannica.com (n.d.); Ghosh (2018)].

In many democratic countries, unfortunately, this hostility to minorities has come through politics. India too has entered a phase where it is acceptable to pander to majoritarian sentiment where, through a rhetoric of demonising the other, a political constituency gets consolidated as an electoral constituency. In such politics there are short term political dividends to be gained even though there is long term damage to the social fabric of society. Again, unfortunately, this politics of aggressive majoritarianism has today become commonplace in many contemporary democracies.[2] It creates situations where it becomes difficult for the general public to accept pluralism as the normal of democratic politics. While acknowledgement by the political class allows the symbols of the minority to become part of the symbolic universe of the nation[3] (one gesture was the French President acknowledging the football World Cup winning French team as the 'rainbow team', representative of all of France)[4] acknowledgment by the general public is also necessary as can be seen in the chant of the Liverpool fans.[5] It also creates spaces for the state to formulate policies that target minorities and respond

[2] Alternative for Deutschland in Germany, Front National in France, Northern League in Italy, Fidesz in Hungary.

[3] This was a point seriously debated at an innovative conference titled 'Living Diversity—Shaping Society' organised by Bertelsmann Stiftung in May 2018. It looked for ways to accommodate the emerging diversities within European societies and finding icons from minority groups was one interesting idea that was considered.

[4] 'It was a moment of communion', former France defender Marcel Desailly, who was born in Accra to Ghanaian parents, told CNN (Grez, 2018).

[5] The presence of Mo Salah in the Liverpool football team during its purple patch produced this chant among the supporters: '*if he's good enough for you, he's good enough for me, if he scores a few, then I'll be Muslim too; if he's good enough for you, then he's good enough for me, if he's sitting in the mosque, that's where I want to be*'.

to their needs. In India, till recently, we have acknowledged such plurality in our laws, institutions, policies and discourse.

Stemming from this acceptance of plurality is the issue of responding to these claims which are sometimes innocuous and easy to deal with and sometimes very hard to accommodate. That is why Nehru in the first decade of Indian independence recognised that minorities could be 'troublesome'. It is the troublesomeness of these minorities, and how to respond to them, which is the second learning that can be gained from the India story. In the first chapter 'Introduction: Pluralism and Democracy' we discussed five scenarios of claims and in the third chapter 'Politics of Minority Accommodation in Postcolonial India' and in the fourth chapter 'Policy Initiatives for Minorities' we detailed the many ways in which India responded to them. We do not wish to repeat the findings here but wish to flag the fact that to accommodate these claims we will need to be open to changing the foundational coordinates of our polity, even those coordinates that have been gained after long decades of struggle.

The India story tells us that plural societies must be willing to enter a zone of negotiation on their core values, such as happened during the unfortunate killings in the Charlie Hebdo controversy in France. Both sides in France had to revisit and reexamine their positions on 'freedom of expression', on the one side, and its limits particularly with respect to 'offending the sacred', on the other. These were apparently intransigent positions and yet to live together peacefully, to co-habit, some middle path had to be found. Fortunately, there is a large body of scholarly literature in political philosophy on pluralism, on overlapping consensus in a context of incommensurable comprehensive doctrines, on representation in the public sphere, etc. which are available to aid this process. In addition to such philosophical resources are many examples of prudence and realism where efforts are made to accommodate minorities in creative ways. The 'European Prize for Urban Public Space' is a good example of such initiatives (Public Spaces, 2019). In India, the writing of history textbooks was an attempt by the government to build in the minds of the young generation a sense of India's cultural plurality. This plural sensibility is unfortunately coming unstuck as the regime in power seeks to cultivate a contrary majoritarian mindset among the young (Amin, 2002). Parallel to the situation in India is the amnesia about the excesses of colonialism that historians in the UK feel is being cultivated by their own history textbooks (Owen, 2016). Museums too are struggling with the challenge of representing their colonial pasts (Birnbaum, 2018; Psaledakis and Lohman, 2018). The second learning from the India story is that to deal with the troublesome decisions of pluralism in the present we have to use multiple resources available to us from debates in political philosophy to innovative urban planning, to historical memory and to the rich resources of the Indian symbolic world.

The third learning from India is that as a polity democratises, a new politics of groups and interests will emerge. Five aspects of this dynamics of democratic politics are worth noting. The first is the growth of non-party political formations, or civil society groups,[6] among minorities that will seek to change the public discourse through the public positions they take that they hope will impact the policies and decisions of the government in power. This is normal politics and must be welcomed even if some of these organisations are overtly partisan and communal. The AIMPLB, SGPC and the CBCI are instances of such non-party political formations. The second is that some of these minority communities, when the demographics are in their favour, may even, in addition to non-party political formations, form political parties to further their agenda. Examples are the Akali Dal in Punjab, the All India Majlis-e-Ittehadul Muslimeen in Telegana and the Indian Union Muslim league in Kerala. These parties, both on the streets and in the legislative chamber, campaign to promote the agenda of their minority group. Their existence should be welcomed and not seen as

[6] We prefer the term non-party political formations because these groups are political even though they may be non-party. The term civil society does not give them a sense of the political and hence is inadequate. This is a point made by D.L. Sheth in his book *At Home with Democracy* (edited by Peter Ronald deSouza).

a communalisation of politics but rather as a secularisation of religion and hence not as a distortion or a deficit of Indian democracy. It is, in fact, an advance of democracy similar to the presence of Christian parties in Europe. The third consequence of this increase in political contestation is the internal contestation which emerges within minority communities, referred to as the demands of 'minorities within minorities' that have begun to challenge the hegemony of the dominant groups. These dominant groups are mostly conservative and resistant to progressive changes within the community especially on the issue of women's rights. Good illustrations of such 'minorities within minorities' which have been very visible and effective are the BMMA, that campaigned against the practice of Triple Talaq (see the chapter 'Politics of Minority Accommodation in Postcolonial India') among Muslims, and the Speak out Against Female Genital Mutilation (FGM) movement within the Bohra community which petitioned the courts to stop FGM (see footnote 38 in the chapter 'Introduction: Pluralism and Democracy'). The fourth aspect of this dynamics of democracy is the aspiration among some groups that were hitherto considered to be part of the majority community, to acquire minority status and thereby get the special advantages that minorities enjoy. This aspiration may be very instrumental, such as getting the benefits minorities get when running educational institutions especially with respect to autonomy in administering such institutions. When groups follow this political route of claiming minority status they present their differences with the majority community as being foundational particularly with respect to scripture, or religious practice, or community norms. In recent years three groups have campaigned to be recognised as minorities by the state that is Lingayats, Ramakrishna Mission and Jains. After due process, minority status was granted only to the Jains who were recognised as a minority religion whereas the other two were seen as being merely sects of Hinduism. This aspiration for minority status should be regarded as a consequence of the democratisation process, an aspect to be welcomed since it adds to the competitive nature of the polity. The fifth and final aspect of this third learning is that the concessions made by the state to minorities results in a push back by the majority community. It is the dark side of the democratisation process in India. We are currently in this phase of push back where because of majority consolidation minorities have had many of their gains reversed.

The fourth learning that has really been the substance of this book, focuses on the accommodation strategy of Indian democracy which developed through distinct laws, institutions, policies and discourse. While the previous three learnings were the product of democratic politics, the demand side of politics, this fourth learning is a product of initiatives from the state, the supply side of politics. These laws, institutions, policies and discourse, must be read as the result of the enlightenment of state leaders, who wanted to make the concessions discussed, and of their prudence, to avoid a discontented citizenry. The place of leaders with vision, passion and a sense of responsibility (Weber, 1946) is often underplayed and the issue of minority rights is a good case through which to compare the vision of two leaders of independent India, the first Prime Minister Jawaharlal Nehru and the current Prime Minister, Narendra Modi.

In India, two aspects of the law, as a domain to accommodate minority claims, need to be noted. The first takes us to the foundational document of the Indian Republic, the Indian Constitution. In the justiciable section on Fundamental Rights, Articles 25–28 which guarantee the freedom of religion and Articles 29–30 which guarantee cultural and educational rights, the Constitution acknowledges the importance of minority concerns and claims. These Articles constitute a statement of the core principles of our democracy. They give minorities the right to practice their religion and also to promote and develop their particular cultures (see the chapter 'Politics of Minority Accommodation in Postcolonial India'). As this guarantee gets embedded in our politics, contestations emerge on what they imply, on what is permitted and proscribed. Such contestations take place in the courts that are central to clarifying and extending the meaning of these constitutional provisions. Many cases have been fought and won, and fought and lost, in the courts on a host of issues such as the freedom of minorities to manage their educational institutions, the practice of divorce in the minority community such as 'triple talaq', the cultural and religious practice of female circumcision, or the denial of the right to inheritance of family property by women (George, 2014; see the chapter 'Politics of Minority Accommodation in Postcolonial India').

The place of courts in expanding the scope of minority rights and thereby making the Indian landscape of rights very contemporary, can be seen in two recent cases of the Indian Supreme Court. These concern the rights of sexual minorities who have fought a long struggle for recognition. Their struggle has yielded some successes.[7]

On 15 April 2014, as a result of several petitions before the Supreme Court of India, a bench comprising Justices Radhakrishnan and Sikri gave a judgement protecting the rights of transgender persons by referring to the fundamental provisions of the constitution. Drawing on a range of resources from case law to historical studies of the colonial origins of sodomy laws, from studies on sex and biology to studies on the psychology

[7] A checklist prepared by an Indian website has offered an interesting list of ten achievements by the LGBTIQ movement in the year 2017. These are: (i) 'Lucknow hosted its first Gay Pride march (the first city in Uttar Pradesh to do so)'. The article suggests that 'people loved it!' an observation difficult to confirm but one far removed from the victim discourse that sometimes accompanies such reports. (ii) Elder LGBTQ members in Mumbai are being offered a safe space to meet for a 'chai and a chat' to tackle loneliness through a social group 'Mumbai Seenagers'. (iii) Tuition fees were scrapped for transgenders at The Manonmaniam Sundaranar University (MSU) in Tamil Nadu. (iv) Parents of LGBTQ individuals crowd-source for a movie on parental acceptance of children. (v) India witnessed its first open transgender wedding and received a whole lot of love online. Here too, the observation that the wedding 'received a whole lot of love online' is similar to the celebratory tone in the first item on the list. (vi) The first formal parent gathering to offer support to the parents of India's LGBTQ members was held in Mumbai. (vii) Indian cinema cast its first transsexual woman as the leading actress, Anjali Ameer. (8) An Indian sub-inspector openly married her same-sex partner in Punjab and the couple was supported by family, friends and colleagues. (ix) Two successful Bollywood movies, Aligarh and Kapoor & Sons, made a lot of people happy for their positive depiction of gay identities. (x) Kochi Metro recruited 23 members of the transgender community (Plummer, 2017).

of the self, from international covenants such as the Yogyakarta declaration to the European Court of Human Rights cases, the Court instructed the state to recognise transgenders (TG) as the 'third gender'. Further, the Court directed the state to accept their right 'to decide for themselves their self-identified gender', to treat them as a socially and educationally backward classes of citizens and thereby to extend reservations to them, to frame social welfare schemes for them, to give them special attention in hospitals and to work to overcome the fear, shame, gender dysphoria and social stigma which they face so that they can 'feel that they are part and parcel of social life and not be treated as untouchables' and so that they 'regain their respect and place in the society which once they enjoyed in our cultural and social life'.[8]

Four years later the Supreme Court, again in response to petitions before it from individuals and social groups, struck down Section 377 of the Indian Penal Code which made homosexuality and sodomy a criminal offence as being 'acts against the laws of nature'. This too was struck down on grounds of discrimination and the fundamental rights of gay persons was recognised.[9] Indian democracy has through these judgements undone decades of injustice against the LGBT communities. The judgements have given the constitutional order new coordinates for co-living with those who have different sexual dispositions from those of the majority. Through innovative readings of the law by the courts this should be seen as a triumph for minority rights.[10]

The second aspect, of crafting institutions to attend to minority claims, is equally educative for those who want to draw lessons from India. There are three aspects of this strategy of using institutions to safeguard minority interests. The first are institutions such as the NMC,

---

[8] Para 129 of judgement delivered on 15 April 2014 at New Delhi.

[9] See the many blogs on the subject at: https://indconlawphil.wordpress.com//?s=377&search=Go

[10] 'Section 377 IPC: Summary Of Four Separate Judgments', https://www.livelaw.in/section-377-ipc-summary-of-judgment-in-4-points/

the NCMEI (see the chapter 'Politics of Minority Accommodation in Postcolonial India'), NMDFC (see the chapter 'Policy Initiatives for Minorities') which are bodies that enjoy either statutory status or get their authority from government orders. These are permanent bodies specifically tasked with attending to the cultural and economic needs of the minority communities. Allied with this is the new Ministry of Minority Affairs that was formed on 29 January 2006. Its functions can be read on the website of the Ministry.[11] It too has a focused agenda and interestingly was formed on the recommendation of the NCM. These institutions serve several purposes. They emerge as sites where minority claims can be sent by the government of the day for attention and advice and as places where minority grievances can be given a public hearing. They are available to regimes that seek consultation on emerging minority demands and they also serve as valuable disseminators to the minority of useful information on government schemes specially made for the minority. The increased off-take of scholarships, from the scheme for students from minority communities, to give them access to better life opportunities through the educational system is a case in point (see the chapter 'Policy Initiatives for Minorities'). In addition, these minority commissions house valuable data for the use of government in its exercise of evidence based policymaking. They also help in monitoring the delivery of schemes to minority groups.

Such special institutions, of course, soon acquire a political logic of their own and may become places of partisan capture by subgroups within the community. This is a risk the democratic system has to take for it has to balance the value of such an institution promoting minority interests with its capture by partisan subgroups. The decision of the NCMEI (as discussed in Chapter 3) in the case of Jamia Millia Islamia can perhaps be seen in this light. The value of NCMEI must, however, be recognised for it shows the importance given by the democratic

---

[11] Ministry of Minority Affairs, Government of India. Available at http://164.100.158.81/ (accessed 18 March 2018).

state to minority education institutions as a specific space to protect the cultural distinctiveness of the minority group. Educational institutions play an important role in socialising students into the elements of minority culture and thereby help in consolidating and transmitting to the next generation the culture of the minority.

The third institution that contributes to strengthening the minority claims are the committees formed by the government to help it to understand what policies to make to increase the minority role in the public sphere and make the polity more inclusive. The Gopal Singh Committee of 1983 and the Sachar Committee, 2005 were such committees. Both committees changed the public discourse on the place of minorities within Indian democracy. The Sachar Committee, because of its research and detailed findings, has been able to give the lie to the argument of the majoritarian forces, that minorities have been regularly appeased by the previous governments, a lie that has taken root in the public mind. The data they produced shows that this is not the case. As a whole the Muslim community is disadvantaged and backward when compared to most other communities (see the chapter 'Policy Initiatives for Minorities'). These three institutions, ministry, commissions and committees should, therefore, be regarded as instruments available to a democratic state to accommodate its minorities. If supported by the government they can play a big role in placing the polity on a certain path (Pierson, 2000).

The third aspect, are the policies that India has followed to accommodate minority claims and interests. These are imaginative and range from the symbolic such as national holidays, to the narrowly material, such as access to finance and loans. These policies can be examined in terms of four distinct groups, those which are: (a) cultural, (b) educational, (c) socioeconomic and (d) affirmative action. These policies that were growing are effective in bringing minorities into the public sphere and making the democracy more inclusive. The presence of members of the minority community in Bollywood and in the Indian cricket team helps in this process of normalisation of plurality in the Indian imaginary. But these policies also run the risk of push back as was the case in some states that were contemplating the idea of giving quotas to backward members of the minority community because they came from the minority community. This was seen as the communalisation of a secular policy. Majoritarian politics has used the myth of minority appeasement to mobilise from the majority community those excluded and denied the benefits of the policy, against the policy and have thereby created hostility to the policy and to the minority community. Politics thereby acquires a communal edge and an adversarial turn.

In conclusion, now let us stand back from the details that we have been examining and return to the general question with which we began the book: What are the relative merits of the two strategies that democratic states have used to make their polities more inclusive, the Indian strategy of a politics of accommodation or the preferred strategy adopted by many European states that require minorities to assimilate and integrate with the larger sections of the society, to become more like them, become French, and not remain as they were, Arab Algerians. The politics of accommodation is based on recognition of cultural difference and of the existence of cultural groups as legitimate entities in politics. In contrast the politics of assimilation is based on downplaying these cultural identities, of ethnic groups qua groups and of emphasising instead their citizenship rights as individual citizens.

Both approaches have merits and demerits. An excess of accommodation can lead to a sense of separateness, even an ethno-nationalism and this can be detrimental to fostering a feeling of cohabitation in a plural society. Ghettos can emerge and the society then becomes a patchwork of communities such as the case of Lebanon. Limited accommodation can also lead to what we have called 'geographies of exclusion' where ghettos also form of sullen communities such as the 'banlieus' in Paris (Misra, 2017). An excess of the demand for integration and assimilation also has the negative effect of migrant communities feeling that they are being asked to give up that which they treasure, that which gives them meaning, their cultural identities. They feel that while they appreciate their life in the host community they also want to keep the identities with which they arrived. The Indian experience has provided many valuable lessons on dealing with cultural diversity while aspiring for an inclusive polity. The European experience too has offered valuable arguments for why individual rights should have the trumping status over other claims. This debate on the relative merits of the two paths needs to continue. This book is a modest attempt at contributing to this debate by presenting the many aspects of the Indian narrative to the larger discourse on inclusive politics in plural societies.

Bibliography

Abreu, Savio. (2009). 'The Making of a Christian Minority', *Seminar*, 602. Available at http://www.india-seminar.com/2009/602/602_savio_abreu.htm (accessed 17 September 2018).

Adams, Richard. (1 February 2018). 'Senior Ofsted Official Backs Headteacher over Hijab Ban for Under Eights', *The Guardian*. Available at http://www.theguardian.com/education/2018/feb/01/ofsted-chief-backs-headteacher-over-hijab-ban-for-under-eights?CMP=Share_iOSApp_Other (accessed 6 February 2018).

Ahmad, Imtiaz (ed.). (1978). *Caste and Social Stratification among Muslims*. New Delhi: Manohar.

Ahmad, Irfan, and Pralay Kanungo (eds). (2019). 'Communal Violence, Electoral Mobilization, and Muslim Representation: Muzaffarnagar 2013–14', in *The Algebra of Warfare-Welfare: Along View of India's 2014 Election*, pp. 163–196. New Delhi: Oxford University Press.

Ahmad, S. Shamim, and A.K. Chakravarti. (1981). 'Some Regional Characteristics of Muslim Caste Systems in India', *Geo Journal*, Vol. 5(1), pp. 55–60.

Ahmed, Hilal. (2014). *Monuments, Memory and Contestation: Muslim Political Discourse in Postcolonial India*. London and New Delhi: Routledge.

———. (2016). 'Representing Muslims in Postcolonial India: Constitution of a Discourse', in *Decolonisation and the Politics of Transition in South Asia*, edited by Sekhar Bandyopadhyay, pp. 348–374. New Delhi: Orient Blackswan.

———. (2018). 'The Politics of Shariat', in *Rethinking Indian Jurisprudence: An Introduction to the Philosophy of Law*, edited by Aakash Singh Rathore and Garima Goswami, pp. 95–103. London and New Delhi: Routledge.

———. (2019). 'Communal Violence, Electoral Mobilization, and Muslim Representation: Muzaffarnagar 2013–14', in *The Algebra of Warfare-Warfare: Along View of India's 2014 Election*, edited by Irfan Ahmad and Pralay Kanungo, pp. 163–196. New Delhi: Oxford University Press.

Aiyer, Mani Shanker. (2006). *Confessions of a Secular Fundamentalist*. New Delhi: Penguin Books.

Alam, M. Sanjeer. (2012). *Religion, Community, and Education: The Case of Rural Bihar*. New Delhi: Oxford University Press.

———. (2014). 'Affirmative Action for Muslims: Arguments, Contentions and Alternatives,' *Studies in Indian Politics*, Vol. 2(2), pp. 215–229.

Ali, Syed. (2002). 'Collective and Elective Ethnicity: Caste among Urban Muslims in India,' *Sociological Forum*, Vol. 17(4), pp. 593–620.

Ambedkar, B.R. (2014). *Dr. Baba Saheb Ambedkar: Writings and Speeches* Vol. 1, edited by Vasant Moon, p. 377. Delhi: Ministry of Social Justice and Empowerment, Government of India.

Amin, Shahid. (2002). 'History Period'. Available at https://www.thehindu.com/thehindu/mag/2002/03/31/stories/2002033100280300.htm (accessed 17 March 2019).

Annamalai, E. (1990). 'Dimensions of Bilingual Education in India,' *New Language Planning Newsletter*, Vol. 4(4), pp. 1–3.

Appadurai, Arjun. (1989). *Number in the Colonial Imagination*, edited by Carol A. Breckenridge and Peter van der Veer. Philadelphia: University of Pennsylvania Press.

Apple, M.W. (1990). *Ideology and Curriculum* (2nd ed.). New York: Routledge and Kegan Paul.

Azad, Maulana Abul Kalam. (1988). *India Wins Freedom.* Delhi: Orient Blackswan.

Baines, J.A. (1893). *General Report on the Census of India 1891*. London: Her Majesty's Stationary Office.

Bajpai, Rochna. (2000). 'Constituent Assembly Debates and Minority Rights,' *Economic and Political Weekly*, Vol. 35(21–22), pp. 1837–1845.

———. (2011). *Debating Difference: Group Rights and Liberal Democracy in India.* New Delhi: Oxford University Press.

Banerjee, B.K., and G. Stober. (2014). 'Living in Harmony? "Casteism", Communalism, and Regionalism in Indian Social Science Textbooks,' *Journal of Educational Media, Memory & Society*, Vol. 6(2), pp. 42–86.

Basant, R. (2007). 'Social, Economic and Educational Conditions of Indian Muslims,' *Economic and Political Weekly*, 10 March, pp. 828–832.

Basant, R., and Abusaleh Shariff. (2010). *Oxford Handbook of Muslims in India.* New Delhi: Oxford University Press.

Batra, Poonam. (2015). 'Curriculum in India: Narratives, Debates, and Deliberative Agenda,' in *Curriculum Studies in India: Intellectual Histories, Present Circumstances*, edited by W.F. Pinar. New York: Palgrave Macmillan.

BBC. (15 May 2017). 'Italian Court Upholds Ban on Sikhs Carrying Knives. Available at https://www.bbc.com/news/world-europe-39928912 (accessed 11 March 2019).

——. (2018). 'Crossing Divides'. Available at https://www.bbc.co.uk/programmes/p063scp6 (accessed 8 March 2019).

Beteille, Andre. (1990). 'Is Job Reservation a Good Policy?' *Seminar*, 375.

Bhargava, Rajeev. (2010). *The Promise of India's Secular Democracy*. New Delhi: Oxford University Press.

Bhasha Research and Publication Centre. (2017). *People's Linguistic Survey of India*. Baroda: Bhasha Research and Publication Centre.

Bhatia, Gautam. (11 May 2017). 'Triple Talaq and the Constitution', *The Hindu*. Available at https://www.thehindu.com/opinion/lead/triple-talaq-and-the-constitution/article18420742.ece (accessed 11 May 2017).

Bhatnagar, G.V. (2018). 'In the Modi Era, Scholarships Granted to Minority Students Dropped Drastically', *Live Mint*, 10 March.

Birnbaum, M. (2018). 'Belgium's Africa Museum Reopens, as Country Confronts its Violent Colonial Past'. Available at https://www.washingtonpost.com/world/europe/this-belgian-museum-needed-a-five-year-overhaul-to-make-it-less-racist/2019/03/14/ef09a106-020e-11e9-958c-0a601226ff6b_story.html (accessed 17 March 2019).

Blackledge, A. (2008). 'Language Ecology and Language Ideology', in *Encyclopedia of Language and Education*, Vol. 9, edited by A. Creese, P. Martin and N.H. Hornberger, pp. 27–40. New York: Springer.

BMMA. (2016). 'No More Talaq Talaq Talaq: Muslim Women Call for Ban on an Un-Islamic Practice'. Available at https://bmmaindia.files.wordpress.com/2016/01/triple-talaq-report.pdf (accessed 16 June 2019).

Bourdieu, P. (1991). 'The Production and Reproduction of Legitimate Language', in *Language and Symbolic Power*, edited by J.B. Thompson, translated by G. Raymond and M. Adamson. Cambridge: Polity Press.

Body-Gendrot. (2010). 'Police Marginality, Racial Logics and Discrimination in the Banlieues of France', *Ethnic and Radical Studies*, Vol. 33(4).

Brass, Paul. ([1974]2005). *Language, Religion and Politics in North India*. London: Cambridge University Press.

——. (1994). *Politics in India since Independence*. Cambridge: Cambridge University Press.

Britannica. (n.d.). 'Srebrenica Massacre'. Available at https://www.britannica.com/event/Srebrenica-massacre (accessed 25 September 2018).

CBCI. (2012). 'Statements of CBCI on Dalit Issue'. Available at http://www.dalitchristianscbci.org/Statements.aspx (accessed 22 September 2018).

——. (2016). 'Policy of Dalit Empowerment in the Catholic Church in India: An Ethical Imperative to Build Inclusive Communities'. Available at https://www.cbci.in/Policies/Policy922172823534.pdf (accessed 14 June 2019).

———. (2018). Available at https://www.cbci.in/about_us.aspx (accessed 17 September 2018).

Chatterjee, Partha. (1994). *Nation and its Fragments: Histories in Colonial and Postcolonial India.* New Delhi: Oxford University Press.

Chatterjee, Debjani. (18 October 2018). 'Sabarimala On Edge A Day After Violence, Women Stopped By Protesters'. Available at https://www.ndtv.com/kerala-news/sabarimala-protests-bandh-in-kerala-protesters-stop-women-from-going-to-sabarimala-protesters-clash-1933780 (accessed 20 June 2019).

Chopra, Ritika. (2011). 'DU Admissions: St Stephen's College Discontinues Dalit Christian Quota'. Available at https://www.indiatoday.in/india/north/story/st-stephens-college-discontinues-dalit-christian-quota-134358-2011-05-25 (accessed 20 June 2019).

———. (2018). 'More Space in School Textbooks for Ancient Indian Knowledge Systems and Tradition', *The Indian Express.* Available at Available at https://indianexpress.com/article/education/ncert-school-books-class-six-to-ten-indian-knowledge-system-tradition-5195025/ (accessed 20 April 2019).

Chrisafis, Angelique. (13 October 2015). 'Pork or Nothing: How School Dinners are Dividing France', *The Guardian.* Available at http://www.theguardian.com/world/2015/oct/13/pork-school-dinners-france-secularism-children-religious-intolerance (accessed 18 July 2018).

Clokie, H. McD. (1936). 'The New Constitution for India'. *The American Political Science Review*, Vol. 30(6), pp. 1152–1165.

Convention on the Rights of the Child, UNICEF. (2018). Available at https://www.unicef.org/child-rights-convention (accessed 4 June 2019).

(The) Communal and Targeted Violence (Access to Justice and Reparations) Bill. (2011) Available at https://www.prsindia.org/uploads/media/draft/NAC%20Draft%20Communal%20Violence%20Bill%202011.pdf (accessed 15 June 2019).

The Constitution of India (official e-version). Available at http://lawmin.nic.in/coi/coiason29July08.pdf (accessed 10 November 2016).

Coupland, R. (1944). *The Indian Problem: Report of the Constitutional Problem in India.* London and New York: Oxford University Press.

Dearden, Lizzie. (26 August 2016). 'Burkini Ban Suspended: French Court Declares Law Forbidding Swimwear Worn by Muslim Women "Clearly Illegal"'. Available at https://www.independent.co.uk/news/world/europe/burkini-ban-french-france-court-suspends-rule-law-forbidding-swimwear-worn-muslim-women-seriously-a7211396.html (accessed 17 July 2018).

Deshpande, Satish. (2008). 'Dalits in Muslims and Christian Communities: A Status Report on Current Social Scientific Knowledge', National Commission for Minorities, Government of India.

deSouza, P.R. (2015). 'Politics of the Uniform Civil Code in India', *Economic and Political Weekly*, Vol. 50(28), pp. 50–57.

———. (2015). 'The Afterlife of the Nehruvian Legacy', *Seminar-India*, 674(October).

——— (21 April 2016). 'Furore over a Handshake Declined in a Swiss Town Holds Valuable Lessons for India', *Scroll.in*. Available at https://scroll.in/article/806868/furore-over-a-handshake-declined-in-a-swiss-town-holds-valuable-lessons-for-india (accessed 10 November 2016).

———. (2018a). *In the Hall of Mirrors: Reflections on Indian Democracy*. New Delhi: Orient Blackswan.

———. (2018b). 'Minority Rights and Democracy in India', entry no 64 in *The Sage Handbook of Political Sociology*, edited by William Outhwaite and Stephen P. Turner, Vol. 1 and 2. London: SAGE.

———. (ed.). (2000) *Contemporary India—Transitions*. New Delhi: SAGE.

DeTocqueville, Alexis. (1964). *Democracy in America*. Bombay: Popular Prakashan.

Dhamija, Ashok. (2012). 'Legal Basis of Haj Subsidy Abolition by Supreme Court'. Available at https://tilakmarg.com/opinion/legal-basis-of-haj-subsidy-abolition-by-supreme-court/ (accessed 20 April 2019).

Dhillon, Gurdarshan Singh. (1974). 'Evolution of the Demand for a Sikh Home Land', *The Indian Journal of Political Science*, Vol. 35(4), pp. 362–373.

Dua, H.R. (1985). *Language Planning in India*. New Delhi: Harnam.

———. (1986). 'Language Planning and Linguistic Minorities', in *Language Planning: Proceedings of an Institute*, edited by E. Annamalai, B. Jernudd and J. Rubin, pp. 43–72. Mysore: Central Institute of Indian Languages.

Dworkin, Ronald. (1997). *In Praise of Theory*, 29 ARIZ. ST. L.J. 353.

Ekbote, G. (1984). *A Nation without a National Language*. Hyderabad: Hindi Prachar Sabha.

Etzioni, Amitai. (2000). 'Toward a Theory of Public Ritual', *Sociological Theory*, Vol. 18(1), pp. 44–59.

——. (2014). 'Communitarianism Revisited', *Journal of Political Ideologies*, Vol. 19(3), pp. 241–260.

Farouqui, Athar. (1994). 'Urdu Education in India: Four Representative States.' *Economic and Political Weekly*, 2 April, pp. 782–789.

Fazal, Tanweer. (2015). *Nation State' and Minority Rights in India: Comparative Perspectives on Muslim and Sikh Identities*. Routledge: London and New York.

Fraser, Nancy. (1990). 'Rethinking the Public Sphere: A Contribution to the Critique of Actually Existing Democracy', *Social Text*, 25/26, pp. 56–80.

Fourth AAE Memorial Lecture full text Freedom of Religion in India-Contemporary Challenges. Available at http://www.csss-isla.com/4th-aae-memorial-lecture-full-text/ (accessed 10 November 2016).

Galanter, M. (1972). 'The Aborted Restoration of "Indigenous" Law in India', *Comparative Studies in Society and History*, Vol. 14(1), pp. 53–70.

——. (1978). 'Who are Other Backward Classes?: An Introduction to a Constitutional Puzzle', *Economic and Political Weekly*, Vol. 13(43–44), pp. 1812–1828.

——. (1984). *Competing Equalities: Law and the backward Classes in India*. New Delhi: Oxford University Press.

Gandhi, M.K. ([1909]1938). *Hind Swaraj or the Indian Home Rule*. Ahmadabad: Navjivan Press.

Gayer, Laurent and Christophe Jafferlot. (2012). 'Introduction', in *Muslims in Indian Cities*, edited by Laurent Gayer and Christophe Jafferlot. Noida: HarperCollins.

General Report on the Census of India. (1891). Her Majesty's Stationary Office, London 1893.

George, Omana. (2014). 'Inheritance Rights of Christian Women since "Mary Roy"'. Available at https://www.livelaw.in/inheritance-rights-christian-women-since-mary-roy/ (accessed 19 March 2019).

Gewirth, Allen. (1996). *The Community of Rights*. Chicago: The University of Chicago Press.

Ghosh, Amitav. (20 December 2018). 'The Ghosts of Mrs Gandhi: Amitav Ghosh Looks Back at the 1984 Massacre of Sikhs'. Available at https://scroll.in/article/906350/the-ghosts-of-mrs-gandhi-amitav-ghosh-looks-back-at-the-1984-massacre-of-sikhs (accessed 18 March 2019).

Gole, Nilofer. (2015). *The Daily Lives of Muslims*. London: Zed Press.

Golwalkar, M.S. (1966). *Bunch of Thought*. Bangalore: Sahitya Sindhu Prakashana.

Gopal, S. (1988). 'Nehru and the Minorities', *Economic and Political Weekly*, Vol. 23, pp. 2463–2466.

Grez, M. (6 July 2018). 'The Fans, Everybody was Together. No Racism, No Discrimination, Everybody was Happy in France', https://edition.cnn.com/2018/06/08/football/france-1998-world-cup-win-anniversary/index.html (accessed 17 March 2019).

Groff, C. (2013). 'Multilingual Discourses and Pedagogy in North India', in *Bilingual Education and Language Policy in the Global South*, edited by J.A. Shoba and F. Chimbutane, pp. 190–206. London: Routledge.

Government of India. (1932). *Report of Indian Franchise Committee*, pp. 175–178. Calcutta: Government of India (Central Publication Branch).

———. (1955). 'The Report of the States Reorganization Commission.' New Delhi: Government of India.

———. (1980). *Report of the Backward Class Commission*, Government of India, Government Press, Delhi.

———. (2007). 'Report of the National Commission on Religious and Linguistic Minorities (NCLRM)'. New Delhi: Government of India.

Government of India Act 1919, Calcutta: N.N. Mitter, Annual Register Office.

Government of India Press. (1953). *Report of the First Backward Classes Commission*, Manager, Government of India Press, Shimla.

Grant, Colin. (2018). 'Britain's Debt to the Windrush Generation'. Available at https://www.nybooks.com/daily/2018/04/24/britains-debt-to-the-windrush-generation/ (accessed 17 March 2019).

Guha, Ramachandra. (2018). 'The Shrinking of St. Stephen's'. Available at https://www.hindustantimes.com/columns/the-shrinking-of-st-stephen-s/story-NkEEHvX9dlOTeqOgqOAz8O.html (accessed 20 June 2019).

Habermas, Jurgen. (2006). 'Religion in Public Sphere', *European Journal of Philosophy*, Vol. 14(1), pp. 1–25.

Hamid, S. (1987). 'Education of Minorities: Future Perspective', *Journal of Educational Planning and Administration*, Vol. 1(2), pp. 211–215.

Hasan, Zoya. (2009). *Politics of Inclusion: Caste, Minorities and Affirmative Action*. New Delhi: Oxford University Press.

Hasan, Zoya, and Ritu Menon. (2004). *Unequal Citizens: A Study of Muslim Women in India*. New Delhi: Oxford University Press.

Hasan, Zoya, and Mushirul Hasan. (2013). 'Assessing UPA Government's Response to Muslim Deprivation' in *Social Development Report*, edited by Zoya Hasan and Mushirul Hasan. New Delhi: Oxford University Press.

Hassan, Sajjad. (2016). 'Survivors of Mass Communal Violence in Muzaffarnagar: Profiles of Loss, Dispossession, and Recovery', in *India Exclusion Report 2015*, pp. 189–205. Delhi: Yoda Press.

Heller, M., and M. Martin-Jones. (2001). *Voices of Authority: Education and Linguistic Difference*. Westport, CT: Ablex.

History.com. (n.d.). 'Rwanda Genocide'. Available at https://www.history.com/topics/africa/rwandan-genocide (accessed 20 June 2019).

Hofverberg, Elin. (26 March 2018). 'Iceland: Bill on Male Circumcision Headed for Review'. Available at http://www.loc.gov/law/foreign-news/article/iceland-bill-on-male-circumcision-headed-for-review/ (accessed 15 July 2018).

Imam, Zafar (ed.). (1978). 'Some Aspects of the Social Structure', in *Muslims in India*, pp. 70–110. New Delhi: Orient Longman.

Jain, A. (1990). *The Making of a Metropolis*. New Delhi: National Book Organisation.

Jayal, Nirija Gopal. (2007). *Representing India: Ethnic Diversity and the Governance of Public Institutions*. New York: Palgrave Macmillan.

Jawaharlal Nehru. (1994). *Selected Works of Jawaharlal Nehru* (SWJN), Second series, General Editor S. Gopal, Vol. 15. Part 2. Vol. 2(10), pp. 521–523. New Delhi: Jawaharlal Nehru Memorial Fund.

Jha, Shefali. (2003). 'Rights versus Representation: Defending Minority Interests in the Constituent Assembly', *Economic and Political Weekly*, Vol. 38(16), pp. 1579–1583.

Jenkins, Laura D. (2000). 'Caste, Class and Islam: Boundaries of Backwardness in India', *The Eastern Anthropologist*, Vol. 53(3–4), pp. 328–339.

Jenkins, Laura D. (2008). 'Legal Limits on Religious Conversion in India', *Law and Contemporary* Problems, Vol. 71(2), pp. 109–127.

Jetly, Rajshree. (2008). 'The Khalistan Movement in India: The Interplay of Politics and State Power', *International Review of Modern Sociology*, Vol. 34(1), pp. 61–75.

Kashyap, Samudra Gupta. (2016). 'Friday to Sunday: Background and Context of Assam's Madrasa Move', *The Indian Express*, 14 December. Available at https://indianexpress.com/article/explained/assam-madrasas-friday-closure-assam-education-minister-himanta-biswa-sharma-4425833/ (accessed 20 April 2019).

Kaviraj, Sudipta. (1997). 'Religion and Identity in India', *Ethnic and Racial Studies*, Vol. 20(2), pp. 325–345.

Khan, J.A., and P. Parvati. (2013). 'Government's Commitment towards Development of Muslims: A Post-Sachar Assessment of Uttar Pradesh and Haryana', in *India: Social Development Report*, edited by Zoya Hasan and Mushirul Hasan. New Delhi: Oxford University Press.

Khan, Borhan Uddin, and Muhammad Mahbubur Rahman. (2009). 'Protection of Minorities: A South Asian Discourse', Eurasia Net, Seventh Framework Programme of the European Commission.

Khalidi, Omar. (2008). 'Hinduising India: Secularism in Practice', *Third World Quarterly*, Vol. 28(8), pp. 1545–1562.

Kirmani, Nida. (2011). 'Mobilising for Muslim Women's Rights in India', *Open Democracy*, 14 January 2011. Available at https://www.opendemocracy.net/en/5050/mobilising-for-muslim-womens-rights-in-india/ (accessed 11 March 2019).

Kothari, Rajni. (1970). *Politics in India*. Delhi: Orient Longman.

———. (1974). 'The Congress System Revisited: A Decennial Review', *Asian Survey*, Vol. 14(12), pp. 1035–1054.

Krishna, Gopal. (1967). 'Electoral Participation and Political Integration', *Economic and Political Weekly*, Vol. 2(3/5), pp. 179–181, 183–185, 187–190.

Kumar, Ashutosh. (2004). 'Electoral Politics in Punjab: Study of Akali Dal', *Economic and Political Weekly*, Vol. 39(14/15), pp. 1515–1520.

Kumar, K. (2000). 'The Problem in Redesigning Curriculum: A Symposium on Working a Framework for School Education', *Seminar*, 493 (September).

Khubchandani, L.M. (1981). *Multilingual Education in India*. Pune: Center for Communication Studies.

Khubchandani, L.M. (2001). 'Language Demography and Language Education' in *Language Education in Multilingual India*, edited by C.J. Daswani. New Delhi: UNESCO.

Kundu, Amitabh. (2014). *Post Sachar Evaluation Committee Report*. Ministry of Minority Affairs, Government of India, New Delhi.

Kymlicka, Will. (1992). 'Two Models of Pluralism and Tolerance,' *Analyse and Kritik*, Vol. 13, pp. 33–56.

——. (2008a). 'The Internationalization of Minority Rights'. *International Journal of Constitutional Law*, Vol. 6(1), pp. 1–32.

——. (2008b). 'Multiculturalism, Social Justice and the Welfare State', in *Social Justice and Public Policy*, edited by Gary Craig, Tania Burchardt and David Gordon. Bristol: The Polity Press.

Lewandowski, S.J. (1984). 'The Built Environment and Cultural Symbolism in Postcolonial Madras', in *The City in Cultural Context*, edited by J.A. Agnew, Mercer J. and D.E. Sopher, pp. 237–254. Boston: Allen and Unwin.

Lewis, M.P., F.S. Gary and D.F. Charles (eds.). (2014). *Ethnologue: Languages of the World* (7th edition). Dallas, TX: SIL International. Available at http://www.ethnologue.com.

Lijphart, Arend. (2004). 'Constitutional Design for Divided Societies', *Journal of Democracy*, Vol. 15(2), pp. 96–109.

Mahajan, Gurpreet. (1999). 'Rethinking Multiculturalism', *Seminar*, p. 484.

Mahmood, Saba. (2015). *Religious Difference in a Secular Age: A Minority Report*. Princeton: Princeton University Press.

Mahmood, Tahir. (2016). *Minorities Commission 1978–2015: Minor Role in Major Affairs* (2nd edition), pp. 129–130. Delhi: Universal.

Mahmood, Tahir. (2010). 'Religion and the Secular State: Indian Perspective', in *Religion and the Secular State: National Reports*, edited by J. Martinez-Torron and W.C. (Jr.) Durham. Provo, UT: Digital Legend Press.

Mill, James. (1826). *The History of British India* (3rd edition). London: Baldwin, Cradock, and Joy.

Mishra, Saurabh. (2011). *Pilgrimage, Politics and Pestilence: The Haj from the Indian Subcontinent, 1890–1920*. New Delhi: Oxford University Press.

Momigliano, Anna. (3 October 2018). 'An Italian Mayor Saved his Village by Welcoming Migrants: Now he's been Arrested for it', *The Washington Post*. Available at https://www.washingtonpost.com/world/2018/10/02/an-italian-mayor-saved-his-village-by-welcoming-migrants-now-hes-been-arrested-it/?noredirect=on&utm_term=.8649e4609dfe (accessed 27 June 2019).

Momin, A.R. (1975). 'Muslim Caste: Theory and Practice', *Economic and Political Weekly*, Vol. 10(14), pp. 580–582.

Margalit, Avishai. (1996). *The Decent Society*, translated by Naomi Goldblum. Harvard University Press.

Martinez-Torron, J., and W.C. (Jr.) Durham. (2010). *Religion and the Secular State: National Reports*. Provo, UT: Digital Legend Press.

Messner, Francis (ed.). (2015). *Public Funding of Religions in Europe*. London: Routledge.

MHRD. (1986). *National Policy on Education*. Department of Education, Ministry of Human Resource Development, Government of India. Available at https://mhrd.gov.in/sites/upload_files/mhrd/files/document-reports/NPE86-mod92.pdf (accessed 15 June 2019).

Misra, Amlendu. (2000). 'Hindu Nationalism and Muslim Minority Rights in India', *International Journal on Minority and Group Rights*, Vol. 7(1), pp. 1–18.

Misra, Manashi. (2016). 'Not On a Friday', *The Indian Express*, 8 December.

Misra, Tanvi. (16 November 2017). 'The Othered Paris'. Available at https://www.citylab.com/equity/2017/11/the-othered-paris/543597/ (accessed 20 April 2019).

Moon, Vasant. (1994). *Dr. Babasaheb Ambedkar: Writings and Speeches*, Vol. 1. Delhi: Dr. Ambedkar Foundation, Ministry of Social Justice & Empowerment, Government of India.

Mondal, Seikrahim. (2003). 'Social Stratification, OBC's and Muslims', *Economic and Political Weekly*, 15 November.

Mukherjee, Hiren. (1993). *The Gentle Colossus: A Study of Jawaharlal Nehru*. New Delhi: Oxford India paperbacks.

Mustafa, Faizan. (2014). *Freedom of Religion in India-Contemporary Challenges*. Available at https://www.religiousfreedominstitute.org/cornerstone/2016/7/19/freedom-of-religious-in-india-current-challenges (accessed 15 June 2019).

Mwere, David. (22 July 2017). 'Kenyans of Indian Descent become 44th Tribe'. *The Daily Nation*. Available at https://www.nation.co.ke/news/Hindu-officially-becomes-Kenya-s-44th-tribe/1056-4027242-12m5ygj/index.html (accessed 22 July 2017).

Nair, Deepa. (2010). 'Textbook Conflicts in South Asia: Politics of Memory and National Identity', *Journal of Educational Media, Memory & Society*, Vol. 2(2), pp. 29–45.

(The) National Integration Conference. (September–October, 1961). Government of India, New Delhi. Available at https://mha.gov.in/sites/default/files/NICBackG-171013.pdf (accessed 17 June 2019).

(The) National Commission for Minorities. (1978). Government of India, New Delhi. Available at https://mha.gov.in/sites/default/files/NICBackG-171013.pdf (accessed 17 June 2019).

National Commission for Minority Educational Institutions (NCMEI), CASE NO. 1443 of 2006.

NCERT. (1975). 'The Curriculum for the Ten-Year School: A Framework. New Delhi: National Council of Educational Research and Training' (NCERT; Publication Department). Available at http://epathshala.nic.in/wp-content/doc/NCF/Pdf/NCF_10_Year_School_eng.pdf (accessed 14 June 2019).

———. (1986). *Fifth All India Education Survey*. New Delhi: NCERT (Publication Division).

———. (1993). *Sixth All India Education Survey*. New Delhi: NCERT (Publication Division).

———. (2000). *National Curriculum Framework for School Education*. New Delhi: NCERT (Publication Department). Available at http://epathshala.nic.in/wp-content/doc/NCF/Pdf/NCF_2000_Eng.pdf (accessed 15 June 2019).

———. (2005). *National Curriculum Framework*. New Delhi: NCERT. Available at http://epathshala.nic.in/wp-content/doc/NCF/Pdf/nf2005.pdf (accessed 20 June 2019).

Nehru, Jawaharlal. ([1946]1994). *The Discovery of India*. New Delhi: Oxford University Press.

———. (1992). *Letters to Chief Ministers*, edited by G. Parthasarthi, Vol. 4 (1954–1957). New Delhi: Oxford University Press.

Newbigin, Eleanor. (2011). 'Personal Law and Citizenship in India's Transition to Independence', *Modern Asian Studies*, Vol. 45(1), pp. 7–32.

Nidhi (2017). 'The Street Names of New Delhi', *International Journal of Academic Research and Development*, Vol. 2, pp. 317–322.

Nigam, Aditya. (2004). 'A Text without Author: Locating Constituent Assembly as Event', *Economic and Political Weekly*, Vol. 39(21), pp. 2107–2113.

Noorani, A.G. (ed.). (2003). *The Muslim of India: A Documentary Record*. New Delhi. Oxford University Press.

———. 2013. 'Patel's Communalism: A Documented Record'. Available at http://www.frontline.in/cover-story/patels-communalisma-documented-record/article5389270.ece?homepage=true (accessed 20 April 2019).

Olusoga, David. (2018). 'The Treasury's Tweet Shows Slavery is still Misunderstood', *The Guardian*, 12 February 2018. Available at https://www.theguardian.com/commentisfree/2018/feb/12/treasury-tweet-slavery-compensate-slave-owners (accessed 14 June 2019).

Oommen, John. (1995). 'Politics of Communalism in Kerala', *Economic and Political Weekly*, Vol. 30(11), pp. 544–547.

Oommen, T.K. (2014). *Social Inclusion in Independent India: Dimensions and Approaches*. New Delhi: Orient Black Swan.

Orange, Richard. (18 December 2018). 'Sweden Democrats: Far Right Takes over Swedish Countryside'. Available at https://www.dw.com/en/sweden-democrats-far-right-takes-over-swedish-countryside/a-46789675 (accessed 8 March 2019).

Osborn, Andrew. (2002). 'Belgium Confronts its Colonial Demons'. Available at https://www.theguardian.com/world/2002/jul/18/congo.andrewosborn (accessed 27 June 2019).

Owen, Jonathan. (22 January 2016). 'British Empire: Students should be Taught Colonialism "Not all Good", say Historians', *The Independent*. Available at https://www.independent.co.uk/news/education/education-news/british-empire-students-should-be-taught-colonialism-not-all-good-say-historians-a6828266.html (accessed 17 March 2019).

Pandey, Gyanendra. (1990). *The Construction of Communalism in Colonial North India*. New Delhi: Oxford University Press.

———. (1999). 'Can a Muslim Be an Indian?', *Comparative Studies in Society and History*, Vol. 41(4), pp. 608–629.

Parekh, Bhikhu. (1996). 'Minority Practices and Principles of Toleration', *International Migration Review*, Vol. 30(1), pp. 251–284.

Parrott, Zach. (13 March 2007). 'Indigenous Peoples in Canada'. *The Canadian Encyclopedia*. Available at https://www.thecanadianencyclopedia.ca/en/article/aboriginal-people (accessed 10 November 2016).

Parthasarthy, G. (ed.) (1985). *Jawaharlal Nehru: Letters to Chief Ministers*, Vol. III. New Delhi: Oxford University Press.

Pattanayak, D.P. (2003). 'Mother Tongue: The Problem of Definition', in *Towards a Multilingual Culture of Education*, edited by A. Ouane. Hamburg: UNESCO Institute of Education.

Pfaff-Czarnecka, Joanna. (2010). '"Minorities-in-Minorities" in South Asian Societies: Between Politics of Diversity and Politics of Difference', in *Minorities in Europe and South Asia*, edited by S.K. Das, pp. 100–131. Kolkata: Samya Publishing Company.

Pierson, Paul. (2000). 'Increasing Returns, Path Dependence, and the Study of Politics', *The American Political Science Review*, Vol. 94(2), pp. 251–267.

Pirie, G.H. (1984). 'Letters, Words, Worlds: The Naming of Sweto', *African Studies*, Vol. 43, pp. 43–51.

Pleasance, Chris. (22 November 2014). 'Children "Black Up" for Traditional Dutch Christmas Festival Despite Growing Controversy in Holland over whether Event is Racist', *Daily Mail Online*. Available at http://www.dailymail.co.uk/news/article-2845589/Children-black-traditional-Dutch-Christmas-festival-despite-growing-controversy-Holland-event-racist.html (accessed 10 November 2016).

Plummer, Lucy. (21 June 2017). '10 Things India's Done Right for Its LGBTQ Community This Year #GayPrideMonth'. Available at https://www.thebetterindia.com/105834/lgbtq-gay-pride-month-india-reasons/ (accessed 20 June 2019).

Prime Minister's High Level Committee. (2006). *Social, Economic and Educational Status of the Muslim Community of India*. Government of India.

PRS. (2019). Available at https://prsindia.org/sites/default/files/bill_files/Citizenship_%28A%29_bill%2C_2016_0.pdf (accessed 16 June 2019).

Psaledakis, Daphne and Isabel Lohman. (December 2018). 'Belgium's Africa Museum Reopens to Confront its Colonial Demons'. Available at https://www.reuters.com/article/us-belgium-museum-africa-idUSKBN1O7003 (accessed 20 June 2019).

Public Spaces. (2019). Available at https://www.publicspace.org/publications

———. (n.d.). Available at http://publicspace.org/en/categories/europe-city-program-1 (accessed 20 June 2019).

Raina, Badri. (12 October 2018). 'Some Puzzling Aspects of the Sabarimala Controversy', *The Wire*. Available at https://thewire.in/women/sabarimala-women-entry-supreme-court-judgement-kerala

Rao, S.S. (2008). 'India's Language Debates and Education of Linguistic Minorities', *Economic and Political Weekly*, Vol. 43(36), pp. 63–69.

Rawls, John. (1987). 'The Idea of an Overlapping Consensus', *Oxford Journal of Legal Studies*, Vol. 7(1), pp. 1–26.

———. (1993). *Political Liberalism*. New York, Columbia University Press.

Report of the Advisory Committee on Minorities. (1947). Constitution Assembly Debate, Vol. 5. Government of India.

Ranalvi, Masooma. (2017). 'Not just India: FGM thrives within America's Dawoodi Bohras too', *The Quint*, 26 April. FGM here means 'female genital mutilation'. Available at http://www.thequint.com/voices/women/female-genital-mutilation-not-just-in-india-dawoodi-bohra-community-practises-in-the-us-too-doctor-arrested (accessed 26 April 2017).

Report of the Christian Missionary Activities Enquiry Committee, Madhya Pradesh (1956). Available at http://voiceofdharma.org/books/ncr/4cmae.htm (accessed 10 November 2016).

Robinson, Rowena. (2005). 'Indian Muslims: The Varied Dimensions of Marginality', *Economic and Political Weekly*, 10 March, pp. 839–843.

Roy, Anupama. (2016). 'Ambivalence of Citizenship in Assam', *Economic and Political Weekly*. Vol. l(26/27), pp. 45–51.

Roy, Kumkum. (2002). 'National Textbooks for the Future?', *Economic and Political Weekly*, Vol. 37(57), pp. 5083–5085.

Rodríguez, Encarnación Gutiérrez. (2018). 'The Coloniality of Migration and the "Refugee Crisis": On the Asylum-Migration Nexus, the Transatlantic White European Settler Colonialism-Migration and Racial Capitalism'. Available at https://refuge.journals.yorku.ca/index.php/refuge/article/viewFile/40483/36472 (accessed 17 March 2019).

Rudolph, Lloyd I., and Susanne H. Rudolph. (1983). 'Rethinking Secularism: Genesis and Implications of the Textbook Controversy, 1977–79', *Pacific Affairs*, Vol. 56(1), pp. 15–37.

———. (1987). *In Pursuit of Lakshami: The Political Economy of Indian State.* New Delhi: Orient Longman.

Ryan, Aidan F. (24 April 2018). 'Two Years After Law School Removed Royall Crest, No New Seal in Sight'. Available at https://www.thecrimson.com/article/2018/4/24/hls-continues-no-seal/ (accessed 21 October 2018).

Sachar, Rajindar. (2006). *Social, Economic and Educational Status of the Muslim Community of India. A Report*. New Delhi: Prime Minister's High Level Committee. Cabinet Secretariat, Government of India.

Sayeed, Saad. (28 April 2018). 'Pakistan's Ahmadi Community Releases Damning Persecution Report'. Available at https://www.reuters.com/article/us-pakistan-religion/pakistans-ahmadi-community-releases-damning-persecution-report-idUSKBN1HZ06R (accessed 17 March 2019).

Sandel, Michel. (1994). 'Political Liberalism—Reviewed by Michael Sandel,' *Harvard Law Review*, Vol. 107(7), pp. 1765–1794.

———. (21 May 2018). 'Right-wing Populism is Rising as Progressive Politics Fails—Is It too Late to Save Democracy?', Available at https://www.newstatesman.com/2018/05/right-wing-populism-rising-progressive-politics-fails-it-too-late-save-democracy (accessed 8 March 2019).

Sarangi, Asha. (2010). *Language and Politics in India.* New Delhi: Oxford University Press.

Schuessler, Jennifer. (2 December 2016). 'Yale Sets Policy that Could Allow Renaming of Calhoun College', *The New York Times*. Available at https://www.nytimes.com/2016/12/02/arts/design/yale-calhoun-college-slavery-debate-policy.html (accessed 17 July 2018).

Shah, G. (2007). 'The Conditions of Muslims', *Economic and Political Weekly*, 10 March, pp. 836–839.

Shakir, Moin. (1972). *Muslims in Free India*. Delhi: Kalamkar Publication.

Shamshi, Shakeel. (2018). 'The Myth of the Haj Subsidy'. Available at https://sabrangindia.in/article/myth-haj-subsidy (accessed 20 April 2019).

Shariff, Abusaleh, and Azra Razzack. (2006). 'Communal Relations and Social Integration' in *India: Social Development Report*. New Delhi: Oxford University Press.

Sharma, K.D. (1978). *Education of a National Minority: A Case of Indian Muslims*. Delhi: Kalamkar Publication.

Sherwood, Harriet. (18 February 2018). 'Iceland Law to Outlaw Male Circumcision Sparks Row over Religious Freedom', *The Guardian*. Available at https://www.theguardian.com/society/2018/feb/18/iceland-ban-male-circumcision-first-european-country (accessed 17 July 2018).

Sheth, D.L. (2009). 'Minority Politics: The Shifting Terms of Policy Discourse', *Seminar*, 602, October.

———. (2018). *At Home with Democracy: A Theory of Indian Politics*, edited by P.R. DeSouza. P.R. Basingstoke: Palgrave Macmillan.

Sherwani, A.R. (1979). 'Educational Backwardness', *Seminar*, 240.

Sikand, Yoginder. (2004). *Islam, Caste and Dalit-Muslim Relations in India*. New Delhi: Global Media Publications.

Singh, B.P., and P.K. Varma. (2001).*The Millennium Book on New Delhi*. New Delhi: Oxford University Press.

Smith, W.C. (1950). 'Hyderabad: Muslim Tragedy', *Middle East Journal*, Vol. 4(1), pp. 27–51.

Sorabjee, Soli J. (2000). 'The Constitutional Order in India: A Framework for Transition', in *Contemporary India—Transitions*, edited by Peter Ronald deSouza. New Delhi: SAGE.

Sridhar, Kamal K. (1996). Language in Education: Minorities and Multilingualism in India,' *International Review of Education/InternationaleZeitschriftFürErziehungswissenschaft/Revue Internationale De L'Education*, Vol. 42(4), pp. 327–347.

Strachey, John. (1894). *India*. London: K. Paul, Trench, Trübner & Co., Ltd.

State of Rajasthan and Ors. vs Vijay Shanti Educational Trust on 21 September, 2001 Equivalent citations: RLW 2003 (4) Raj 2568.

Stump, R.W. (1988). 'ToponomicCommemoration of National Figures: The Case of Kennedy and King', *Names*, Vol. 36, pp. 203–216.

Tejani, S. (2013). 'Between Inequality and Identity: The Indian Constituent Assembly and Religious Difference, 1946–50', *South Asia Research*, Vol. 33(3), pp. 205–221.

The Anand Marriage Act, 1909. Available at https://indiankanoon.org/doc/125344553/ (accessed 19 September 2018).

The Guardian. 2018. 'The Guardian View on the Windrush Generation: The Scandal isn't Over'. Available at https://www.theguardian.com/commentisfree/2018/oct/17/the-guardian-view-on-the-windrush-generation-the-scandal-isnt-over (accessed 27 June 2019).

———. Available at https://www.theguardian.com/world/2002/jul/18/congo.andrewosborn (accessed 17 July 2018).

———. (2018). 'Egypt Attack: Gunmen Kill Seven Coptic Christians in Bus Ambush'. Available at https://www.theguardian.com/world/2018/nov/03/egypt-attack-gunmen-kill-coptic-christians-bus-ambush (accessed 17 March 2019).

The Indian Express (24 February 2015). 'RSS Chief Mohan Bhagwat Targets Mother Teresa, Says Conversion was Main Objective Behind her Service'. Available at https://indianexpress.com/article/india/india-others/conversion-was-behind-mother-teresas-service-says-rss-chief-bhagwat/ (accessed 5 April 2018).

The New York Times. (15 March 2019). 'Jacinda Ardern Consoles Families After New Zealand Shooting'. Available at https://www.nytimes.com/2019/03/15/world/asia/new-zealand-shooting.html (accessed 17 March 2019).

The Sikh Gurudwara Act, 1925. Available at http://www.lawsofindia.org/pdf/haryana/1925/1925HR8.pdf (accessed 19 September 2018).

The Report of the Advisory Committee on Minorities. (1947). Available at http://164.100.47.194/Loksabha/Debates/cadebadvsearch.aspx (accessed 20 June 2019).

Trivedi, Divya. (2014). 'Saffron Slant', *Frontline*, 3 October 2014.

Tully, James. (2000). 'Struggles over Recognition and Distribution', *Constellations*, Vol. 7(4), pp. 469–482.

Varshney, Ashutosh. (2002). *Ethnic Conflict and Civic Life: Hindus and Muslims in India*. New Haven, CT: Yale University Press.

Vasudevan, Hari. (2018). 'Not by Book', *Indian Express*, 15 June.

Vatsyayan, Kapila. (1972). *Some Aspects of Cultural Policy in India*. Paris: UNESCO.

Vijayan, Suchitra. (28 August 2017). 'How the Triple Talaq Judgement was in Many Ways a Wasted Opportunity', *Scroll*. Available at https://scroll.in/article/848521/how-the-triple-talaq-judgement-was-in-many-ways-a-wasted-opportunity (accessed 28 August 2017).

Wagner, Adam. (15 June 2011). 'Ban Male Circumcision? No, Scientific Evidence of Harm is not Strong Enough', *The Guardian*. Available at https://www.theguardian.com/law/2011/jun/15/male-circumsion-ban-health-religion-debate (accessed 6 February 2018).

Walzer, Michael. (1990). 'The Communitarian Critique of Liberalism', *Political Theory*, Vol. 18(1), pp. 6–23.

Watson, Keith. (1979). 'Educational Policies in Multicultural Societies', *Comparative Education*, Vol. 15(1), pp. 17–31.

Weber, Max. (1946). 'Politics as a Vocation', in *From Max Weber: Essays in Sociology*, edited by Hans Gerth and C. Wright Mills. New York: Oxford University Press.

Weiner, Myron. (1983). 'Political Consequences of Preferential Policies: A Comparative Perspective', *Comparative Politics*, Vol. 16(1), pp. 35–52.

Weisskopf, T.E. (2004). *Affirmative Action in the United States and India: A Comparative*. London: Routledge.

Whelan, Y. (2005). 'Mapping Meanings in the Cultural Landscape', in *Senses of Place, Senses of Time*, edited by G.J. Ashworth. Berlington: Ashgate Publishing Company.

WHO. (2016). Available at http://www.who.int/mediacentre/factsheets/fs241.en/ (accessed 10 November 2016).

Williams, Rina Verma. (2006). *Postcolonial Politics and Personal Laws: Colonial Legal Legacies and the Indian State*. New Delhi: Oxford University Press.

Willsher, Kim. (2010). 'France Urged to Repay Haiti Billions Paid for its Independence'. *The Guardian*, 15 August 2010. Available at https://www.theguardian.com/world/2010/aug/15/france-haiti-independence-debt (accessed 14 June 2019).

Wright, Theodore P. Jr. (1997). 'A New Demand for Muslim Reservation in India', *Asian Survey*, Vol. 37(9), pp. 852–858.

Yeoh, Brenda S.A. (1996). 'Street-Naming and Nation-Building: Toponomic Inscriptions of Nationhood in Singapore', *Area*, Vol. 28(3), pp. 298–307.

Young, Iris Marion. (1995). 'Rawls's Political Liberalism', *Journal of Political Philosophy*, Vol. 3(2), pp. 181–190.

Zakaria, Rafiq. (1995). *The Widening Divide: An Insight into Hindu-Muslim Relations*. New Delhi: Penguin.

Zerilli, Linda M.G. (2012). 'Value Pluralism and the Problem of Judgment: Farewell to Public Reason', *Political Theory*, Vol. 40(1), pp. 6–31.

Zelinsky, W. (1983). 'Nationalism in the American Place Name Cover', *Names*, Vol. 31, pp. 1–28.

Index

Note: The letter 'n', 't' following locators refers to footnotes, tables respectively.

About the Authors

Peter Ronald deSouza is a professor at the Centre for the Study of Developing Societies (CSDS), New Delhi. He was the director of the Indian Institute of Advanced Study (IIAS), Shimla, where he served two terms from 2007 till 2013. He was with the Goa University, Department of Political Science, from 1987 to 2003. His area of research is on democratic politics in South Asia. He is the author of *In the Hall of Mirrors: Reflections on Indian Democracy* and has edited *At Home with Democracy: A Theory of Indian Politics.*

Hilal Ahmed is an associate professor at CSDS, New Delhi. He works on political Islam, Muslim modernities/representation and the politics of symbols in South Asia. His book *Muslim Political Discourse in Postcolonial India: Monuments, Memory, Contestation* looks at these thematic concerns to make sense of the nature of contemporary Muslim political discourse. He has also authored *Siyasi Muslims: A Story of Political Islams in India*, where he presents an evocative story of politics and Islam in India that goes beyond the given narratives of Muslim victimhood and Islamic separation.

Mohd. Sanjeer Alam is an associate professor at CSDS, New Delhi. He works on a variety of themes including socio-spatial inequities in education, social exclusion, affirmative action and electoral politics (Muslim politics in particular). His major work is the book titled *Religion, Community, and Education: The Case of Rural Bihar.* Along with K.C. Sivaramakrishnan, he has co-edited *Fixing Electoral Boundaries in India: Processes, Outcomes and Implications for Political Representation.*

